Landscapes of the
COSTA
BLANCA

a countryside guide

John and Christine Oldfield

SUNFLOWER
BOOKS

First published 1997
by Sunflower Books
12 Kendrick Mews
London SW7 3HG, UK

ISBN 1-85691-090-3

Well at Caprala (Walk 24)

Important note to the reader

We have tried to ensure that the descriptions and maps in this book are error-free at press date. The book will be updated, where necessary, whenever future printings permit. It will be very helpful for us to receive your comments (sent in care of the publishers, please) for the updating of future printings.

We also rely on those who use this book — especially walkers — to take along a good supply of common sense when they explore. Conditions change fairly rapidly in these mountains, and *storm damage or bulldozing may make a route unsafe at any time.* If the route is not as we outline it here, and your way ahead is not secure, return to the point of departure. *Never attempt to complete a tour or walk under hazardous conditions!* Please read carefully the notes on pages 39 to 44, as well as the introductory comments at the beginning of each tour and walk (regarding road conditions, equipment, grade, distances and time, etc). Explore *safely*, while at the same time respecting the beauty of the countryside.

Cover photograph: Approaching the first mill on the Camí de l'Escaleta (Walk 17)
Title page: The Caballo Verde ('Green Horse') rises beyond almond blossom (Car tours 1 and 3)

Photographs by the authors
Touring map by John Theasby and Pat Underwood
Walking maps adapted from Spanish military maps, with kind permission of the Servicio Geográfico del Ejército
A CIP catalogue record for this book is available from the British Library.
Printed and bound in Great Britain by Brightsea Press, Exeter

10 9 8 7 6 5 4 3 2 1

❀ Contents

Left: Almond groves below Aixorta (Car tour 3). Below: Cherry orchards near L'Orxa, with Benicadell rising in the distance (Car tour 2)

✿ Preface

For many years Spain has occupied a special place in our hearts and minds. Wherever our work has taken us we have always looked back nostalgically on the years we lived there, missing the mountains, the relaxed way of life and that special *ambiente* we find hard to describe. In the mid-80s we spent three years in Mallorca and now, many holidays and about ten years later we are back, this time in the old Kingdom of Valencia. The Costa Blanca forms a large part of this region and, as with Mallorca, it is not all fish and chips, discos and organised coach trips. Travel only a short distance inland, and the bustle of the resorts is left far behind. You find yourself surrounded by market gardens, orchards and orange groves, while the dark rugged silhouettes of the sierras beckon you close.

We heed that call as often as we can and never tire of the feeling of belonging which envelops us as we set foot in the mountains. Here we can put aside the stress and hassle of modern living. From the humblest daisy to the most exotic orchid, wild flowers create a vision of delight; the air is filled with the scent of fragrant herbs; birdsong drifts along on the breeze; mountain peaks dominate the skyline; weather-beaten faces of villagers in the fields break into smiles as you pass; all these images combine to create the *ambiente* we find irresistible.

We hope, with this book, to persuade those who might otherwise not stray from the coastal strip to venture into the countryside. Even from the coast, the mountains in the distance look impressive; but the rocky cliffs, deep gorges *(barrancos)*, fertile valleys, and little villages clinging to the slopes can only be fully appreciated from close quarters. This is the purpose of the car tours. As you drive, your feet will surely itch to be out walking, so take advantage of the picnic suggestions — usually only a short distance from a suitable parking spot, they often provide the opportunity for a nearby stroll. Better still, if you are even just reasonably fit, try some of the longer walks in the book. We have attempted, in our grading of each walk, to give you enough information to judge its suitability to your level of fitness. Shorter, generally easier, walks are also suggested. While touring you will pass close to the starting points of the walks and will, hopefully, be tempted to try one, perhaps the next day.

Walkers tend to be quite possessive about their mountains, and we are no exception. To come across several other groups of people each time we venture out would spoil our sense of solitude. But the mountains of the Costa Blanca are so vast, and the paths through them so plentiful, that we are happy to share our walks with you — there is room for all of us!

— JOHN AND CHRISTINE OLDFIELD

Acknowledgements

We are grateful to the Centro Excursionista de Valencia, who have provided information and allowed us to delve into their resources. Without their publications and informal route guides, we would never have discovered some of the fascinating places that we introduce to you in this book. The work of Rafael Cebrián is particularly appreciated. We would also like to thank Eric Wright for sharing some of his local knowledge with us, and for his hospitality. The pleasant company and assistance of Ross Gow, while checking the accuracy of our walk descriptions, was much appreciated.

Language, place names and glossary

Many people on the tourist beat speak English, but that is not the case when you leave the coast. A simple Spanish phrase book or pocket dictionary can be invaluable — although many older people speak Valenciano and are uncomfortable with Spanish.

In the Costa Blanca region you will quickly become aware that place names may have two different spellings — **Castellano** (Spanish as we know it) and **Valenciano**. Mostly the two are very similar, with just an omitted letter or added accent, but in a few cases they can be quite different. The popular revival of Valenciano means that Castilian names are gradually being changed on signposts and maps. But some towns and features are known only by their Castilian names, and are likely to remain so. In this book we have used the version we feel you are most likely to encounter, but give both versions where confusion might occur.

Some of the older settlements have rather long names, but it is customary to abbreviate them. We have used full names once only. For

---

SNOW WELLS *(casas de nieve, neveras, pous, cavas, cavetas)*
Several of our walks feature well-preserved *pous* or *cavas*, and you will be amazed by their size and the solidity of their construction.

Before the days of the refrigerator, snow was commercially 'harvested', compacted in a well and left till summer, when it was cut into blocks of ice. During the coolest time of the day, usually in the hours of darkness, the ice was transported down the mountains by mule, donkey or cart, to the distant centres of population. These wells are described by different names, depending on their location — for example those on the Carrasqueta Ridge are called *pous,* while those around Agres are called *cavas*.

High in the mountains, walls were built in strategic locations to catch the drifting snow and, whenever there had been a significant fall, men would be hired to shovel it into a *pou* and press it down.

instance, after mentioning Planes de la Baronía, we refer to it thereafter simply as Planes. There are many place names beginning with 'Beni', for example Benialí, Benirrama, Benitaia. These are relics of the Moorish occupation, the prefix being comparable to the Scottish 'Mac'.

In the course of the text, where it 'felt right', we have used some local words instead of the English equivalent. In the glossary below we give their meaning.

ambiente atmosphere
arroyo stream
autovía dual carriageway
ayuntamiento, ajuntament town hall
barra French stick, baguette
barranco, barranc gorge, ravine, gully
bocadillo sandwich (often half a *barra*)
bodega wine cellar/shop
cabo, cap cape
calle, carrer street
camino, camí small street, path
camino rural country road
canaleta small water channel
casa/casita house/little house
castillo, castell castle
cava/caveta snow well (see below)
Castellano see Language, page 6
cerro hill
coll, collado hill or saddle
corral farm
correos post office
coto privado de caza private hunting reserve
cueva, cova cave
embalse reservoir
ermita hermitage or chapel

finca farmhouse and farm
fuente, font spring
gasoleo diesel
gasolina petrol
hostal cheap hotel
hoya, foia valley, basin
huerta market garden
lavadero wash-house
levante east
masía, mas farm
mirador viewpoint
molino, molí windmill
nao ship
nevera snow well (see below)
peña, penya rock
piscina swimming pool
playa, platja beach
plaza square
pou snow well (see below)
puerto mountain pass or seaport
puig mountain
río river
salinas saltpans
santuario sanctuary or hermitage
tapas snacks or appetizers
torrente dry river bed
turrón almond sweetmeat
Valenciano see Language, page 6
valle, vall valley
vuelta circuit

Caveta del Buitre (Walk 19)

These *pous* were sometimes just natural dips in the ground but, more often, were specially constructed for the purpose. Pits were dug, usually cylindrical in form, and when full of snow were covered with brushwood and branches to ward off the worst of the summer heat. More sophisticated wells were covered by a stone hut with a conical roof and two or three access doors. Stone steps or iron rungs would be set into the walls of the pit to enable the pressers and block-cutters to get down to the snow level, and special tools were used to cut the blocks.

❀ Getting about

There is a reasonable bus service between the main centres on the coast and some of the larger inland towns, but in the mountain regions bus times are not designed to suit walkers. However, it is possible to reach some of our walks by **bus**, and we have included the relevant timetables on pages 133-134. Timetables can vary, depending on the season, so visit local bus stations for up-to-date information (tourist offices in this area do not keep bus timetables). A few walks are also accessible by **train** or by El Trenet (timetable page 133). El Trenet (sometimes called El Limonero or the 'Lemon Express') runs up and down the coast between Denia and Alicante, stopping at every imaginable place en route and affording leisurely views of coastline and countryside. For some of the walks you could make use of a **taxi**, or arrange to stay overnight close to the area where they start.

The most practical option is to **hire a car**. This way you are free to stop at will to admire a view, fill up water bottles at roadside *fonts,* or explore some of the fascinating villages through which you will pass. Cars can be hired at reasonable prices through travel firms when booking flights. Alternatively, in the coastal towns, there are many companies vying for business with special offers and discounts. Make sure you know exactly what you are paying for before hiring; the price quoted may not include collision damage waiver or unlimited mileage.

BENIDORM

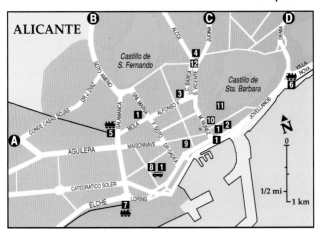

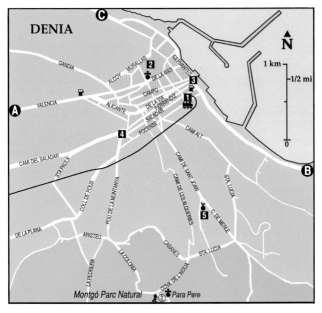

BENIDORM KEY
1 Tourist office
2 Town hall
3 Police
4 Market
5 Railway station
6 Albir buses
7 UBESA buses
8 Guadalest buses
9 Pl. de la Hispanidad

ALICANTE KEY
1 Tourist offices
2 Town hall
3 Market
4 Street market
5 RENFE railway station
6 FGV railway station
7 Murcia railway station
8 Bus station
9 Post office

10 Cathedral
11 Museum
12 Plaza España

DENIA KEY
1 Railway station and
  tourist information
2 Denia castle
3 Cruz Roja (Red Cross)
4 MAPFRE roundabout
5 Mosque

❀ Picnicking

We have found some spectacular picnic spots during our walks through the mountains in this area of Spain. They should appeal to those of you who prefer *very* short walks. If you are car touring, they are an 'off-the-beaten-track' alternative to the area's designated picnic sites, mostly by the roadside, with benches and bins (indicated in the touring notes with the symbol ⊼). These tend to get quite busy on Sundays and *fiestas*. How much better it is to get away from the trappings of civilisation and enjoy a picnic in the wilderness, watching a stream flow by, admiring a mountain view or listening to the birds!

All the information you need to find these more secluded picnic spots is given below, where *picnic numbers correspond to walk numbers,* so that you can quickly find their general location by looking at the touring map (where walks are outlined in white). We give you walking times and transport details. The precise location of the picnic spot is indicated by the symbol *P* on the appropriate *walking map,* which also shows the nearest 🚗 parking place and 🚌 stop (if accessible by bus).

Please remember to **wear sensible shoes** and **take a sunhat.** It's a good idea to take a plastic groundsheet as well, in case it's damp or prickly.

A country code for walkers, motorists and picnickers

The Spanish countryside is essentially unspoiled. It is only around the more accessible, and therefore popular, picnic or camping areas that you will come across litter. Please do not be tempted to add to it. Fire is a major hazard in countryside that is always parched during the summer months (and sometimes all year round after a drought). Respect this country code and ensure that this beautiful area remains unspoiled.

- **Take all your litter away with you.**
- **Do not light fires or throw away cigarette ends.**
- **Protect all wild and cultivated plants.** Don't pick wild flowers. Never cross cultivated land, and do not be tempted to pick cherries, citrus fruits, almonds or olives — these are clearly someone's private property.

Montgó from the trig point on Cabo San Martín (Walk 2c — and just a short stroll from the setting for Picnic 2c)

Take food *with you* for picnics; don't rely on buying it en route. There are few shops in the villages, and their range is quite limited. A fresh *barra*, a hunk of cheese, a couple of tomatoes and some fresh fruit make a satisfying feast. We always carry a small sharp knife, salt and serviettes, to avoid making up sandwiches in advance.

At some of the picnic sites there are *fonts*, so you can enjoy a refreshing cool drink with your food and refill your water bottles. But after long droughts and in the height of summer some *fonts* might run dry; do not *rely* on them as your only source of liquid on a trip. And, of course, leave no rubbish behind, even if others have done so before you.

All picnickers should heed the country code below.

- **Do not disturb or frighten animals or birds.**
- **Protect water sources.** *Fonts* (springs) in the mountains are especially important. When attending to 'calls of nature' keep well away from springs and streams, and make sure that you bury all paper.
- **Walkers — do not take risks!** Never walk alone and always tell someone where you are going and when you expect to return. It might be helpful also to leave this information on a note in your hotel room. Remember that any route could become dangerous after storms or bulldozing. If you are lost or injured you may have to wait a long time for help. *Deep gorges* should always be treated with care and caution. Walkers have disappeared or died in the mountains of the Costa Blanca. Usually the cause of these accidents is carelessness and lack of common sense.

2b JAVEA'S *MOLINOS* (map pages 48-49, photograph page 50)

🚌 car or taxi to the Santuario de Nuestra Señora de Los Angeles on the Cap de San Antonio road (Car tour 1); 21min on foot from the Santuario, or 12min if you drive up to the crest (limited parking). Walk up Camí del Monastir, then follow Walk 2b from the 25min-point (page 48). No shade, but rocky plinths to sit on and fantastic views across Jávea Bay.

2c CRUZ DEL PORTICHOL (map pages 48-49, photograph page 11)

🚌 by car or taxi from Jávea (Car tour 1); 4min or 21min on foot. Follow Walk 2c (page 47) for 4min, to picnic on the grassy terraces or at the cliff edge. Shade of pines if you want it, magnificent views, lovely ambience. Or follow Walk 2c for about 10min, then take the eroded path on the left which leads to steps down to Cala Sardinera (21min), a secluded pebbly beach, with clear water for a swim. No shade.

4 SIERRA DE CORTINA (map page 55)

🚌 by car or taxi from Benidorm (Car tours 1 and 4); 10min on foot. Follow Walk 4 (page 55) for 10min. There is a shady area on the left under pines just before reaching the saddle. But if you prefer views and don't mind sitting in the full sun, turn left from the saddle and head towards the northern peak of Cortina; in 3min reach the concrete foundations of an old *casita*. This serves as an excellent table.

5 PUNTA DE LA ESCALETA, SIERRA HELADA (map pages 56-57)

🚌 by car, taxi or on foot to Benidorm's Playa Levante (Car tour 1). You can either drive to within 200m of the picnic spot, or follow coastal paths for 40min. Follow Short walk 5-2 (page 56). This rocky promontory offers no shade, but there are magnificent views round the coast to Benidorm. You could also follow a path up to the 17th-century *torre*, to look out to the cliffs of the Sierra Helada.

6a, b SERPIS RIVER (map pages 60-61)

🚌 to L'Orxa station (Car tour 2); either 12min or 46min on foot. (a) Follow Walk 6 (page 59) for 9min, then take the track to the right. In a few minutes you will come to abandoned grassy terraces on the

Picnic 10b: The lavadero at Fleix

left, a pleasant spot overlooking the river, with shade from old olive trees. (b) Follow the walk to the 46min-point, then turn right to the low dam. Sit on the dam wall, listen to the sound of running water and watch the fish swimming. There is some shade nearby.

8a, b   THE ENCHANTED POOLS (map page 67)

🚗 to the 18km marker, about 2km east of Planes, on the C3311 (Car tour 2); 16min or 31min on foot. (a) Follow Walk 8 (page 65) as far as the pools (16min 🍴). Refresh yourself with the cool water or just sit on the steps. There is a *font* nearby and shade from the sides of the gorge. (b) For a more natural spot, continue as far as the small reservoir (31min). Shade, running water, rocks to sit on and 'English meadow' atmosphere.

10a   THE EBO RIVER (map pages 70-71)

🚗 to Vall d'Ebo (the 33km point on Car tour 2); 20min on foot (or only 8min, if you drive to the cemetery). Follow Walk 10 from the 3h30min-point (page 76). Choose your spot by the river, at its best when flowing. Little shade but flat rocks, deep pools and the beautiful sound of running water. Alternatively continue up to Font Xili. Shade, stone seats, views over valley and hills and fresh, clear water from the *font*.

10b-d   VALL DE LAGUART (map pages 70-71, photographs opposite and pages 72-73)

🚗 to Fleix (Car tour 1); 5-45min on foot. Follow Alternative walk 10 (page 73). (b) Picnic at the *lavadero* shown opposite (5min; stone seats, font, shade) or, for more spectacular settings, also with shade: (c) descend steeply down the Mozarabic trail shown on pages 72-73, to the cave and waterfall (30min); (d) go all the way down to the floor of the Río Ebo (45min).

11a, b   FINCA BIJAUCA and CASA TANCAT (map pages 78-79)

🚗 to the AV1203 near Tárbena (Car tours 1 and 3); 8min or 30min on foot. Follow Walk 11 (page 77). (a) At 8min the grassy area beside Finca Bijauca has terrace walls to sit on, shade if you want it and fantastic views. If you venture into the longer grass in the summer be aware of the possibility of snakes. (b) At the 14min-point, fork left and descend steeply into the valley, where an old house, surrounded by cherry trees, is an idyllic and secluded setting overlooked by rugged peaks and the high cliffs of Paso Tancat. (This is the 2h53min-point on the main walk.)

12a, b   FONTS DE L'ALGAR (map pages 78-79, photograph page 82)

🚗 to Fonts de l'Algar (Car tour 1); no walking, or 43min on foot. Follow 'How to get there' at the top of Walk 12 (page 81), to park at Casa Federico. (a) On weekdays out of season it is very quiet here, and you can sit at the side of the pools, by the little waterfalls (no shade). (b) Follow Short walk 12 and picnic on the rocks by the waterfall, a playground for small birds. Plenty of shady trees.

13a, b   FONT MOLI (map pages 86-87) 🍴

🚗 to Benimantell (Car tour 3); no walking, or 10min on foot. Follow 'How to get there' at the top of Walk 13 (page 85), to park at Font Molí. (a) Here there is a *font* and picnic benches on two levels — but little shade. (b) For a more inspiring spot make a start on Walk 13 and at the 6min-point take the track straight ahead, to a flat shaded area (10min). There are two rickety picnic tables, or take a blanket and sit on the ground overlooking the valley and the mountains to the north.

15 EMBALSE DE GUADALEST (map pages 86-87)

⌂ to Beniardá (Car tour 3); 6min on foot. Follow directions in the car tour (page 28), to drive through the village to the gateway down to the river. Sit on the pebbly beach or walk a little away from the reservoir, to where flat rocks and shady trees provide a more sheltered spot (6min).

18a BARRANC DEL SINC (map pages 100-101, photograph page 103)

⌂ to Alcoi (Car tour 4); 8min on foot. Follow 'How to get there' at the top of Walk 18 to park near the brickworks. Then follow the walk for 8min. Delightful area beside the cobbled path and steps which lead up the *barranco*. There are rocks to sit on, and the towering cliffs provide plenty of shade. After heavy rains there will be water in the *barranco*.

18b, c SANT CRISTOFOL (map pages 100-101) ⌂

⌂ to Cocentaina (Car tour 4); no walking, or 25min on foot. (b) At the traffic lights, just before leaving the town, turn left to Sant Cristófol, and drive up to this *zona recreativa* (about 1km). The large terraced complex has an attractive picnic and barbecue area as well as a *font*, some caves, a *mirador*, a bar-restaurant and plenty of shade. (c) Drive *past* the picnic site and continue up the concrete road to a *mirador* just below Cocentaina castle. A path leads to the castle in about 10min, but for the picnic spot turn sharp right at the *mirador* and follow Alternative walk 18 (but in reverse) for 25min — to an idyllic setting under the cliff, on the top terrace of almond and olive groves. There is shade, rocks and planks to sit on and magnificent views over to Serrella and Aitana.

19 ERMITA DE LA MARE DE DEU (map pages 100-101) ⌂

⌂ to Agres (Car tour 4) and follow signs to the *ermita* and convent; no walking. There is a bar-restaurant here, but the nearby picnic benches are in a beautiful setting, with views over the Agres valley. Shade, *font*.

20 FONT MARIOLA (map pages 100-101) ⌂

⌂ to Font Mariola (Car tour 4); no walking. See Car tour 4 at the 100km-point (page 32), to drive to the *font*. It could be busy here in season and at weekends, but otherwise this is an idyllic spot. There are benches, ample shade, a large water tank and a little *canaleta* running by.

21 FONT ROJA (map pages 114-115, photograph page 113) ⌂

⌂ to the Parque Natural de Font Roja (optional detour at the 55km-point on Car tour 4); no walking. Extensive picnic areas in the pines, with benches, barbecue areas, water, bar/restaurant. Heavily wooded, with several signposted walks. Avoid on Sundays or in high season.

22 PENAGUILA CASTLE VIEW (map page 118)

⌂ to Casa Alta on the A171 about 3km out of Penáguila (Car tour 4); 10min on foot. Follow Walk 22 from the 24min-point (page 117) as far as the crest. This rocky vantage point is in full sun, but views of the castle and surrounding mountains and valleys are breathtaking.

23a POU DEL SURDO (map page 121, photograph page 118)

🚌 or ⌂ (Car tour 4) to Puerto de la Carrasqueta; 23min on foot. Follow Walk 23 (page 119) as far as the *pou*. There is plenty to explore, an old snow well, some shade if you want it, and fine views.

23b MAS DE LA COVA (map page 121)

⊟ to La Sarga (Car tour 4); no walking necessary but, for the agile, there is an optional climb up to some prehistoric cave paintings. Park at Mas de la Cova (see the 136km-point on page 34). The house is uninhabited, but its fields still cultivated. A peaceful spot, some shady trees and places to sit. On the hillside, overhanging rocks shelter caves containing prehistoric paintings, and the path to them can be seen clearly from here. It is steep and narrow and it will take about 10min to negotiate.

24 RAMBLA DELS MOLINS (map on reverse of touring map)

⊟ to the Catí-Petrer road (see Car tour 5 after 93km; page 38); up to 20min on foot. Follow Walk 24 (page 122) from the 3h14min-point, from the restaurant down into the river bed. A particularly spectacular setting under steep sandy cliffs is reached after about 16min. Oleanders grow along the river bed, there are rocks to sit on and shade if required.

25a FORGOTTEN FINCA (map on reverse of touring map, photograph below)

⊟ to Castalla (Car tour 5); 50min on foot (or 35min if you drive as far as Fam, Fum y Fret). See 'How to get there' at the top of Walk 25 (page 126), then follow the Short walk to the *finca* shown below. A secluded spot overlooking the Castalla valley, with shade and plenty to explore.

25b CATI ERMITA (map on reverse of touring map)

⊟ to Xorret de Catí (Car tour 5 after 86km); 20min on foot. From the hotel head south on the road (walkers' signpost PR-V29). After 2min turn left uphill on a track. Pass the large Casa de la Administración on your right, with a nearby *nevera* (9min). At a junction of tracks (15min) go right; this leads to the *ermita*. Fabulous far-reaching views over El Cid and the Sierra de Maigmó. Shade in surrounding pine woods.

26 CAMI DE SAN JUAN (map on reverse of touring map)

⊟ to the 29km marker on the A211 (Car tour 5); 19min on foot. Follow Walk 26 along the old trail to the first hunting boundary marker. Sit on the ground at the edge of almond groves and look across to the Sierra de la Argueña. Pines afford shade; herbs scent the air.

The 'forgotten finca' *(Picnic 25a) is worth exploring — it has a functioning well, an old* canaleta, *and (about 50m/yds behind the house) a large underground tunnel.*

Touring

Our five car tours cover the northern and central parts of Alicante Province. Each tour begins from one of the major tourist towns on the coast; wherever you are based, the starting point is easily accessible.

There are **three main types of road** in this part of the country. The A7 *autopista*, or motorway, which runs north to south is the quickest way to travel between coastal towns. However, it is a toll road and quite expensive. The parallel N332 tends to become congested even outside the tourist season and progress can be slow. Some of our tours follow parts of the N340, the main inland road which runs north from Alicante, and it presents few traffic problems. Other roads tend to be narrow and, in the mountains, rather winding. They carry relatively little traffic, but what traffic there is might well be travelling in the middle of the road ... and going either very fast or very slowly. *Take great care at all times and expect the unexpected.* There is a great deal of road construction and upgrading going on in the area, and road numbers do change. We have tried to give sufficient instructions to ensure that this causes only minor irritation.

Many of the towns or villages on the tours are well worth exploring, whether to visit their museums, study their architecture or just to absorb their atmosphere. We recommend that you **park somewhere suitable and continue on foot**, particularly through the older quarters. Streets were built to accommodate pedestrians or donkey carts, not motor vehicles; even in the smallest of cars you may find yourself in a very 'tight spot'.

Our touring notes are brief, giving only the minimum of historical detail. Instead we place emphasis on times and distances, road conditions and possibilities for sightseeing, **picnicking** and **walking**. During a long car tour you may encounter a landscape which you would like to explore at leisure another day.

Our touring times allow for no stops or

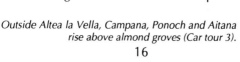

Outside Altea la Vella, Campana, Ponoch and Aitana rise above almond groves (Car tour 3).

16

detours and, of course, assume driving within the speed limit. **The pull-out touring map is designed to be held out opposite the touring notes; symbols** on the map correspond to those in the text. On main roads you will find that **petrol stations** are plentiful; in the mountains some of the small villages have a pump (well signposted and open during normal business hours).

When touring *do* make sure that you always carry **plenty of water**. A car can become very hot and uncomfortable in the sunshine, and there is not always a convenient bar just where you might want one. If you intend stopping en route to buy **food**, remember to do so before shops close up for their extended lunch break. All the towns and most of the villages you will pass through have bars. Those that don't provide full meals usually have a selection of *tapas* or can make up a *bocadillo*. Bars and petrol stations are likely to have toilets and telephone.

In winter it can be cold and windy in the mountains so take adequate **warm clothing**. Whatever the time of year, **the sun can be strong**. Suncream and head covering are a must if you wander in the villages, stop for a picnic or take a stroll. Even with our long experience of Spain, we are sometimes surprised at the strength of the sun.

Allow plenty of time for the tours. You will derive little pleasure from rushing from place to place. The pace of life, especially in rural Spain, is slow, and you will do well to imitate it. Stop and explore or investigate things that catch your eye. We have found that it is often purely by chance that we stumble on something quite delightful.

Please heed the country code on pages 10-11.

1 COSTA BLANCA NEW AND OLD

**Benidorm • Cap de la Nao • Jávea • Cap de San Antonio
• Denia • Orba • Fleix • Fonts de l'Algar • Benidorm**

179km/111mi; 4-5 hours' driving; exit C from Benidorm (plan page 8)

On route: ⌘ at Peñón de Ifach, Cap de San Antonio, Cueva de las
Calavares, Fonts de l'Algar, Polop, La Nucia; Picnics (see *P* symbol and
pages 10-15): 2b, 2c, 4, 5, 10b-d, 11, 12; Walks 1-5, 10, 11, 12, 16

*If you have time for only one car tour this is the one to do. The heavily-
populated, affluent coastal strip is picturesque and fascinating, con-
trasting starkly with the landscape presented as you turn in towards the
mountains. Then you are suddenly confronted with vast open spaces,
layer upon layer of sierras, tiny villages clinging to hillsides and picture-
postcard views of mountain peaks. This is the real Costa Blanca, and
we hope that it whets your appetite for exploring on foot.*

Leave Benidorm from Rincón de l'Oix, at the eastern end
of Playa Levante: take the northbound Avenida Ametlla
de Mar. (To the right at this junction is the road to *P*5 and
the start of Walk 5). After 3km turn right for Playa de Albir.
The road runs through orange groves, parallel with the
Sierra Helada — its ridge looking quite benign from this
side. Turn right for Playa de Albir again (7km); after about
0.5km you pass the road where Walk 5 brings you from
the Sierra Helada into **Albir** (8km ✗). Continue through
the town on the main road, close to the shore, following
signs for Altea. The Albir lighthouse stands out prominently at the end of the sierra, while ahead, behind Altea
church, is the flattish-topped mountain of Oltá, focus of
Walk 3.

In **Altea** (10km ✝ ⛰ ✗ ⛟) drive past the yacht and fish-
ing harbours, and take the road along the seafront. Then
turn left up to the parallel main road (N332) whenever
you wish (it may depend on traffic). Pass
palm-fringed villas hidden behind walls
dripping with bougainvilleas and cross the
estuary of the Algar and Guadalest rivers,
before reaching a crest. Below are the
moorings of a private yacht club and, ahead,
the remains of Calpe Castle high on a peak
at the end of the Sierra de Toix.

Immediately after passing through the
Mascarat tunnels a closer view of Oltá presents itself ahead and soon afterwards the
Peñón de Ifach comes into sight. At 22km
take the turn-off right for Calpe Sur. (Just
beyond the turn, a road goes up to the left to

*The Peñón de Ifach rises 360m/1200ft above the
Salinas de Calpe. Taken from Oltá (Walk 3)*

18

the railway station, starting point for Walk 3.) Enter **Calpe** (24km ⬚✝⛰✖🖳⊕) and follow the main road downhill, heading towards the Peñón de Ifach. Apart from this amazing rock (see below) and a couple of good beaches, Calpe also has its own *salinas* — salt pools — which are just to the left of the road (25km). You will notice flamingos and gulls as you drive by, but a short stroll will also reveal many waders. At the end of the *salinas* turn right and follow signs to the Peñón de Ifach. Park where you can, just before the information boards (could be very busy in the summer). If you have time, climb to the top, but in any case leave your car for a while and admire the views of the Sierra Helada and Calpe Bay (🚏📷).

Return to the *salinas* and turn right towards Playa Levante, parallel with the sea. Oltá rises on your left. Stop at the *mirador* (31km 📷) for views of Cap de Moraira, the Peñón de Ifach and the coast. Pass the beach resorts of Benissa, itself situated a few kilometres inland. After cresting a rise, you return to sea level, passing promenade gardens. After winding through the main street of **Moraira** (40km ✖🖳), you rise slightly to a roundabout. Turn left on the AV1342 for Teulada, curling above healthy vineyards. At a fork (42km) go right for Benitachell and Jávea (AV1349). Land developers seem to be taking over the area around **Alcassar**. Antennas crown the Cumbre del Sol on the right before you enter **Benitachell** (45km).

Turn right on the AV1341 for Jávea, then go right again (47km) on a road signposted only 'Restaurante El Campo'. On the descent vineyards gradually give way to almonds.

Pass El Campo and The Inn on the Green (there are several golf courses in this area). On coming to a T-junction at Residencia Pinasol, turn left and follow the road as it sweeps round to the right, past some villas, and descends steeply to a crossroads (51km). Turn right past the Restaurante Carrasco and join the main Cap de la Nao road (AV1331). Continue through woods and between vines and almond trees until you come to a right-hand bend where a cross, the Cruz del Portichol, overlooks the coast. This viewpoint (55km 🔂) is the starting point for **P**2c and Walks 2c to Cabo San Martín and 2d to Cala Portichol (in summer, parking could be difficult). Continue winding up the hill where yet more development threatens to spoil this heavily-wooded area. Pass a turn off right to Granadella (57km), a secluded cove (Walk 2e). The road becomes more built-up and descends to the lighthouse of **Cap de la Nao★** (59km ✕🔂). There are superb coastal views from the *mirador.*

Turn round, go back to the AV1331 and follow signposting for Jávea. Views are quite different from this new perspective. The rocky mass of Montgó (photograph page 11) immediately dominates the skyline ahead, becoming ever more impressive as you draw nearer. Ignore a left turn to Benitachell (67km) and, on reaching the outskirts of **Jávea** (71km ⛄🏔✕⊡⊕M; Walk 2a) turn left. Pass the Día supermarket and then Mercadona, both on the left. At the roundabout go straight on and follow the one-way system uphill, then turn right for Denia and Cap de San Antonio. This is the Carretera de Denia (A132) which zigzags up and out of Jávea. Just after you leave the town boundary you will see the Ermita de Santa Lucia (⛄) atop a hill to your left and, a little further on, an entrance to the Parque Natural del Montgó. Soon afterwards turn right (74km) for Cap de San Antonio. The road takes you through pleasant wooded countryside, past villas and haciendas and, on the right, the imposing Santuario de Nuestra Señora de los Angeles (⛄; parking for **P**2b). A couple of kilometres further on, Walk 2b starts at the *zona recreativa* on the left (🅿). The road then crests the hill, opening up views of Cap de San Antonio lighthouse and over the coast to Cap de la Nao and Jávea Bay. From the *mirador* just before **Cap de San Antonio★** lighthouse (78km 🔂) admire the majestic cliffs of the headland visited in Walk 2a.

Return to the A132, turn right and drive around the base of Montgó. Just past the Campo de Tiro (shooting range; 82km), the road reaches a crest from where, on a clear day, you can see all the way to Valencia and beyond, with Denia in the foreground. At this point there is another entrance to the Parque Natural.

From here the road winds down into **Denia** (◻†▲▲△✕ ◙⊕M; see plan on page 9). Go straight on at the round-about and through the outer suburbs to the promenade (87km). The A132 continues past the harbour to the large 'Cruz Roja' roundabout. You want to go left here, but to do so you must first circle the Red Cross building, before taking the appropriate exit past the petrol station (◙). Note the railway station off to the left, follow the one-way system to the left and then take the first right into Passeig de Saladar, a wide road mostly taken up by a palm-lined central reservation and many parked cars. Turn left at the second crossroads (just after Bar Noelia), cross the railway and go straight ahead up Camí de Sant Joan, heading for Montgó. Fork right at the Al Khalif mosque, then turn right into Assagador de Santa Lucia (92km). At an open area take the left fork signed to Pare Pere (93km). This quite pretty and ornate Franciscan *ermita* is still in use and is a popular place for visitors.

Continue past the *ermita* as the road winds downhill. It becomes Carretera de la Colonia and is badly potholed in places, but perfectly drivable — with care. Straight-away you will pass, on the left, the Denia entrance to the Parque Natural del Montgó. Walk 1 starts here. The road winds down to a junction where you turn left into Assagador de las Cabanes (later Pou de la Muntanya); this takes you through a housing estate, with views of Denia castle ahead. Cross the railway line back into Denia and go straight on at the next junction. At the MAPFRE round-about, take the exit past the MAPFRE building signposted to San Carlos hospital. Keep on this road, following the Alicante signs, past the Campsa station (◙), and go straight on at the next four roundabouts. You have now left Denia and should take the well-signposted slip road into **La Xara** (99km). Pedreguer, your next destination, is signposted straight ahead on the A131.

Drive through La Xara, heading for the hills and away from the tourist beat. Now you can relax a little and enjoy the gentle rural countryside, old villages perched on hillsides and some spectacular mountains. Pass through groves of oranges and date palms before reaching a set of traffic lights. Go straight across and into **Pedreguer** (105km). Take the right turn for Parcent, then go right again for Orba (AV1411). As you drive through a fertile valley, the old sturdy *fincas* make a change from white villas, and the sierras ahead give you a taste of what is to come. Rounding a bend just after some picnic benches (110km ⊞), come to the Cueva de las Calaveras★, where prehistoric remains are to be seen along with stalactites, stalagmites and rock domes over 20m/65ft high.

In **Benidoleig** (111km) keep straight on towards Orba. Ahead is the Vall de Laguart and rising to the left the sierra shown on page 1, Caballo Verde (Green Horse). Depending on which account you read, the ridge was named for its physical appearance or after a Moorish knight who used to appear there on a green horse to defend his territory. At **Orba** (115km ▢♣✕) drive straight ahead towards the church. Turn left by the church, then go right for Fontilles. At the junction, go straight ahead on the AV1433. Wind up through olive groves and citrus orchards, with magnificent views (▣) of the surrounding sierras and valleys. At a junction (118km), take the left fork (AV1432) signposted to Fontilles. Notice the defile created by the Ebo River, clearly visible in the valley to the right. You soon pass the road to the Sanatorio de Fontilles, a leper colony dating from 1909. It is also a research centre. The road ascends, with stunning panoramas (▣), into the Vall de Laguart, through **Campell** and up to **Fleix** (122km). Continue up the road. If you have waited till now to picnic, park at the school — the starting point for Walk 10. A few metres up the road, where it continues to Benimaurell, take the track off right. You can picnic at the *lavadero* shown on page 12 or follow the Mozarabic trail shown on pages 72-73 down to a cave, a waterfall and the valley floor (*P*10b-d).

Return through Fleix and Campell, gaining intermittent views of Orba castle perched prominently on top of a crag. At the entrance to Orba (128km), turn right on the C3318 for Benidorm (129km ⛽). Contour around the slopes, then zigzag uphill. You will get closer views of Orba castle from here with the impressive peaks of Caballo Verde to its left. The road then descends through olive groves, crosses the Jalón River and climbs again. Just after the 15km marker, notice the isolated building, with a pine tree in front, set up on the saddle ahead to the left — the restaurant on the Coll de Rates. At **Parcent** (133km ♣✕) the road heads right towards Tárbena and winds steeply uphill. *Miradors* (▣ 138km; 140.5km) give fantastic views over the valley.

From the Coll de Rates (540m/1770ft; 141km ✕) the road descends above the Barranco de Vinarreal in what locals call the Tárbena valley. It is surrounded by astonishing sierras, and on a clear day the views are breathtaking. You might see choughs playing around the rocky slopes and cavorting over the valley as the road undulates through terraced hillsides, giving a fresh view at every turn. Pass the AV1203 off right (148km) to the start of Walk 11 (and ***P***11) and continue into **Tárbena** (149km ✕). Then wind down to another *mirador* (152km 📷), from where you can see the amazing Bolulla Castle (🏰) stuck on its crag — and also down to Benidorm.

Continue to descend steeply, passing sheer crags and deep gorges, the most impressive being the Paso Tancat, to **Bolulla** (156km). As you leave the village, Penya Severino, the culmination of the Bernia Ridge, dominates the view to the left and does so all the way down to the Algar Valley. Blessed with a great deal of underground water, this valley is one of the most fertile in the area.

Turn left (159km) on the road signposted to **Fonts de l'Algar★** (✕ΑΔΜ) and, 1km downhill, look for the restaurant Casa Federico on the left: out of season you will be able to use its car park, which is just alongside some attractive pools (***P***12a). Walk 12 starts here, as does the short walk to ***P***12b (photograph page 82). In high season, continue up through the development to the main car park at the top of the hill. The complex, with waterfalls, *fonts* and other attractions, is worth exploring.

Returning to the main road (C3318) continue into **Callosa d'En Sarriá** (165km ✝⛪✕⛽⊕M). At the roundabout in the centre go left on the C3318, signposted to Benidorm. Less than 1km along to the right is the start of Walk 16 in the beautiful setting shown on page 95. Cross the Guadalest River (167km) and soon Campana comes into view, towering ahead of you. Drive through **Polop** (169km), past gardens (Α) on the right. You might like to stop briefly in Polop to look at its fountain which has 221 spouts and is decorated in tiles representing the shields of all the administrative areas of Alicante. Continue along a crescent-shaped 'esplanade' road, lined with a lighted walkway with blue walls, into **La Nucia** (170km). Leaving La Nucia (Α) the Sierra Helada again looms into view. Pass a road off right to Finestrat (177km); it leads to ***P***4 and the start of Walk 4 along the Sierra de Cortina. Follow the road all the way back into Benidorm (179km) and use the plan (page 8) to find the best route back to your hotel.

2 NORTHERN VALLEYS — THE CHERRY ROUTE

Denia • Pego • Planes de la Baronía • Beniarrés • L'Orxa • Vall de Gallinera • L'Atzubia • Denia

120km/74mi; just over 3 hours' driving; exit A from Denia (plan page 9)

On route: ⍴ at the lime kilns, Alcalá, L'Orxa; Picnics (see **P** symbol and pages 10-15): 6, 8, 10a; Walks 6-9

This tour is probably the most scenic in the area. It follows the northern valleys where every available plot of land is cultivated. While orange, almond and olive trees abound, the abundant cherry trees leave the most lasting impression. The area is particularly attractive after spring rains, when it is lusciously green, and the trees are in full blossom. You will have spectacular views of surrounding sierras, including the unusual horned peaks of the Sierra de Benicadell. Enjoy them, but take care on the many bends in the narrow valley roads. Some motorists may find the sheer drops on several stretches unnerving. Once you enter the mountains, Planes is the only place where petrol is available.

L eave Denia by Exit A (signposted 'Autovía', 'Alicante'), meeting the main Alicante-Valencia N332 road after 9km, in Ondara. Turn right towards Valencia, then, after 1km, go left on the C3311 for Pego. Almost immediately cross the Greenwich Meridian, indicated by a large sign. Pego is directly ahead, nestling at the foot of the mountains, its church prominent against the hillside. It is an important town and might well be called the 'gateway to the mountains'. Shortly after entering **Pego** (20km ⌂✝ 🏔 ✕🅿⊕) turn left at the roundabout and zigzag through the outskirts following signs for Sagra and Callosa. Watch for the 1km marker and, just beyond it (21km) turn right on the AV1431 for Vall d'Ebo, winding steeply up a narrow road through pine woods. After about 5km there are magnificent views (📷) over Pego deep in the valley, overlooked by its castle high on a hill. You are right in the heart of the mountains, enjoying spectacular scenery.

After rounding the hillsides, the road climbs to a pass (29km), with an old converted windmill on the right. Just over the crest a deep gorge, the Barranco del Infierno, cuts through the barren mountains (📷). Descend through market gardens and orchards. On the approach to Vall d'Ebo you cross a blue-painted bridge (33km). About 30m straight ahead there is a road to the left where you could park, to take a stroll along the river (*P*10a). But the tour turns right on the AP1042 and bypasses **Vall d'Ebo** (✝✕ ⊕△), following the river in the opposite direction.

Turn right across another bridge and drive out of the valley, past a huge cave, the Cova del Rull★ (36km). Soon the natural rock arch at the end of the Sierra de Foradá comes into sight ahead. Then, in a sheltered spot just before another bridge, you encounter the first of the many

24

cherry orchards. Cross the high plateau, the road lined in places with sage, rosemary and thyme (sorry, no parsley!) and the air alive with flocks of goldfinch. Make a stop at 43km to visit the ancient lime kilns (⌂) and a *nevera* (snow well), then continue past **Alcalá de la Jovada** (44km ⌂Δ). Both Vall d'Ebo and Alcalá have vastly reduced populations now, but originally formed an important part of the territory of the legendary Moorish ruler known as Al Azraq. This cherry route was all part of his 13th-century 'kingdom', and many of the terraced lands you see owe their structure to the Moors he ruled.

Pass by the village of **Margarida** (∎✕), then turn left (50km) on the C3311 (the Vall de Gallinera road), passing the Venta de Margarida. Just after crossing the Pont de les Calderes (53km), opposite the 18km marker, a narrow road leads to the Barranco de la Encantada (Walk 8). Why not park on the left about 100m past the bridge and take a walk along the *barranco* (**P**8)? Continue to **Planes de la Baronía** (⌂♦✕⌸Δ), overlooked by the Ermita de Santo Cristo. If you need petrol you must drive into Planes and fill up. The village is worth a detour in any case, to see its setting around the medieval castle and old aqueduct which still serves the wash-house.

But the main tour bypasses Planes: just after the petrol sign, turn right on the AP1007 for Beniarrés (54km). This little road descends steeply into the valley. As you climb out the other side, notice steps on the right to the *ermita* (♦) high above. On the left catch sight of a reservoir, the Embalse de Beniarrés, and the village's little white church standing prominently on top of a hill, with Benicadell rising majestically behind it (photograph page 66). The road descends to the *embalse,* where we have seen osprey, herons, cormorants, ducks and other waterbirds. Cross the dam (60km) and continue round the other side to **Beniarrés** (64km ♦). When you reach the junction with the AP1001 turn right and drive past the village following the wide valley of the river Serpis towards L'Orxa (Lorcha). The valley, heavily wooded and cultivated (more cherries), is green throughout the year and the high mountain ahead of you is Safor, climbed in Walk 7.

Just as you approach a bridge over the river Serpis, a road on your left leads 0.5km uphill to the old railway station shown on page 63, starting point for Walk 6 through the Serpis Valley. Cross the bridge and turn right (71km) into **L'Orxa** (72km ⌂⌂), at the end of the Serpis Gorge and protected by the Castell de Perputxent (**P**6;

photograph below). Walk 7 starts at Font Grota (⊼), at the entrance to the village, in a garden on your right. Drive past the village, alongside the dry river bed. Just where the road looks as if it is running out, turn left, away from the village. You wind very steeply up to the ridge behind L'Orxa. This new, narrow road is not on many maps, but the surface is good, and the views of Benicadell off to the right are eyecatching (photograph page 4). Drive past terraces all the way to the top, then head across the flat-topped ridge to a junction and a STOP sign (78km). Turn right, and descend towards the Sierra de Foradá.

Very tight hairpin bends take you into the **Vall de Gallinera**. Cross a ford (usually dry) and turn left to **Al-patró** (82km). Here rejoin the C3311, turning left towards Pego. Almond and orange orchards grace the terraces, but soon it becomes evident that each little village along this route derives its living from the abundant cherry trees. In the spring you'll be surrounded by the beauty and fragrance of the blossom; in summer you can stop and buy the fruit. The road runs high above the *barranco* and there are some fantastic views down the Gallinera Valley (83km 📷). You pass through the little settlements of **La Carroja** (✗), **Benissivá** and **Benialí**. The turret of Gallinera Castle (Walk 9, photograph page 69) comes into view on top of a hill ahead, and steep cliffs close in on either side as you leave the valley.

The countryside eventually opens out again into terraced orchards surrounding **L'Atzu-bia** (97km), where Walk 9 begins, and Pego comes into view straight ahead. Soon after entering **Pego** (101km), follow signs for Denia, skirting the centre of Pego. At the round-about, continue on the C3311 through **Verger** back to Denia (120km).

Perputxent Castle (Picnic 6). This impressive fortress was initially the stronghold of Al Azraq before being reconquered by Jaime I. It subsequently came into the hands of the Knights Templar, was confiscated and came under the power of Jaime II. It then passed to the new Orden Militar de Santa María de Montesa.

3 CENTRAL VALLEYS — THE ALMOND ROUTE

Calpe • Callosa d'En Sarriá • Guadalest • Confrides •
Gorga • Castell de Castells • Jalón • Calpe

131km/81mi; 3-4 hours' driving from Calpe

On route: 🚌 at Callosa, Quatretondeta, Castell de Castells; Picnics (see
P symbol and pages 10-15): 11, 13, 15; Walks 3, 11, 13, 15, 16

Mountains surround you on the outward route through the picturesque
Guadalest Valley and on the return along a narrow, winding road
through the Jalón Valley. Almond groves are a major feature of the land-
scape: in January and February large areas are ablaze with pink and
white blossom. But at any time, the variety of scenery provided by the
two valleys with their surrounding sierras makes this tour unforgettable.

Leave Calpe (Walk 3) from the Plaza Central. Drive up
the hill following signs to Alicante and join the N332
going south. Every bit of land has been developed for
housing. Calpe Castle is prominent as you continue under
the railway line, down into the Mascarat Gorge and
through three tunnels cut from the sheer rock of the
mountainside. Take the right fork signposted Callosa d'En
Sarriá (9km), then turn right again for Callosa and go
under the A7 motorway past a petrol station (10km ⛽).

You are now on the C3313 and almost immediately
going through **Altea la Vella**, an upmarket residential area
situated just under the Bernia Ridge. Take in the amazing
views shown on pages 16-17, of Campana, Ponoch and
the Sierra de Aitana, ahead and to the left, as you drive
through seemingly endless citrus groves. In stark contrast
to the barren mountains, the countryside stretching out
at either side of the road is lush and green. As well as the
more common fruit and nut trees there are large groves
of *nísperos* (medlars), easily distinguished by their much
denser and darker foliage.

At the roundabout in the centre of **Callosa d'En Sarriá**
(19km ⛽🏔🍴⛽⊕M) take the exit to Alcoi and Guadalest
(still the C3313). At the 1km road marker (20km) you pass
the brickworks where Walk 16 begins — in the gorgeous
landscape shown on page 95. The road (🚌) skirts high
above the Guadalest with fantastic views encompassing
the valley and Guadalest Castle. Just before crossing the
river (🍴) the sierras of Aixorta and Serrella dominate the
landscape (photograph page 92), as the road winds quite
steeply uphill. On rounding the bend, just after a bar with
a commanding view of the valley, enjoy your first close-
up of the remains of Guadalest Castle perched on top of
its rocky outcrop. Further round, houses come into view,
clinging precariously to the slopes below the castle. As
you pass a rather grand drystone wall and a *mirador*
(28km 📷), the buttresses of Penya Mulero (Walk 13),

27

much favoured by golden eagles, rise on the left.

Pass a road off to the right (30km) to the Embalse de Guadalest; it leads to the start of Walk 15. **Guadalest★** (31km ⌂✕M🗗) is a one-street village of scarcely 200 inhabitants. But in summer it is bristling with tourists on account of its superb setting. The rocks rise up alongside the road and the *mirador* (🗗) at the castle affords a magnificent panorama of the surrounding sierras. As you drive through the village you enjoy a first view of Confrides Castle in the distance. Ignore the turn-off left to Benidorm. On entering **Benimantell** (✕) you pass a turn-off left to El Trestellador restaurant (33km); Walk 13 starts about 1.5km up this road (*P*13). Turn right (34km AV1036) and descend to **Beniardá**. Zigzag through its incredibly narrow streets, following the signs to the Piscina Municipal. Turn down right in front of the rather ornate Casa Consistorial in the tiny main square. As you leave the village the road bears left but, if you want to stretch your legs, park around here and take the track off to the right on the bend (through a gate marked with a red dot). This will take you down to the banks of the Guadalest (*P*15; photograph page 90).

Set off again and, after passing the swimming pool, cross a small bridge (37km). Turn left immediately and drive alongside the river. When the road forks, go right. This narrow, winding road is somewhat rough in places, so take it easy. Pass a pumping station, cross the now dry river, and navigate a short unsurfaced, but not difficult, section. As you enter **Abdet** (42km) turn left at the junction and drive straight through. You are now on the wide AV1035. Turn right at the main C3313 which takes you through **Confrides** (45km ⌂✝▲✕). The road then climbs past the Rincón del Olvido (Corner of Oblivion) and through a pass (966m; 49km ✕🗗), before descending into the next valley. The hills ahead, being less rocky, are more gentle, and there are many paths ribboning up the slopes which are wooded or terraced almost to the tops.

Continue through **Benasau** (56km ✝✕). Cocentaina Castle (⌂) stands out on the stark hillside ahead just before you turn right on the A103 (59km) for Gorga. This road undulates through pretty rural countryside to **Gorga** (63km), where it takes a sharp right turn (AP1033) towards Quatretondeta. You are now heading eastwards again on the northern side of the Sierra de Serrella; the soft rock makes for some unusual formations. Drive across several bridges which span a series of shallow gorges before winding up past **Quatretondeta** (68km ▲ ✕ ⌓).

As the narrow road contours round the slopes watch for small birds. Some will only be summer visitors, but the chirpy serins with their yellow flashes abound in the fruit trees all year. When you join the A120 at **Facheca**, a little village tucked into the hillside (73km), turn right and pass the old village of **Famorca** (76km). The road, now wider but still winding, crosses more dry river beds. The spectacular Sierra de Aixorta becomes visible ahead, with Serrella Castle on a peak to its right (📷 81km). Wind gradually downhill towards picturesque **Castell de Castells** (84km ╪▲✕), nestling in the valley below. Just before entering the village, turn right at the bridge (⌓) towards Tárbena. Park by the picnic tables, if you wish to explore Castell de Castells, a maze of narrow streets.

Then continue along the winding, poorly-surfaced AV1203, in the setting shown on page 4 (left). Just past the 3km road marker (93km) a track to the right marks the start of Walk 11 (*P*11). The long ridge of Ferrer and the rugged peaks of Bernia rise on the left. On the outskirts of **Tárbena** (96km ✕) turn left on the C3318. The road affords views into the Vinarreal Valley (Walk 12) as it contours to the Coll de Rates (540m/1770ft; 103km ✕). Wind down into the Jalón Valley, past two viewpoints (📷 103.5km, 106km), towards **Parcent** (110km ╪✕). Just before this village, which is dominated by its church, turn right on the A142 for Alcalalí. Almond groves lead the eye to the Sierra del Caballo Verde (photograph page 1). Just after entering **Alcalalí** (113km ✕) turn right on the AV1421 (a sign indicates ⊕ 3km away).

Jalón★ (116km ╪▲✕⊕) is very much given over to expatriates and tourists. Many of the streets (and the dry river bed) are lined with flea-market stalls on Saturdays; restaurants and *bodegas* abound. As the road bears right, avoiding the centre, look up the little streets to the left and catch glimpses of the old town and the blue dome of the small church. Climb out of the valley, through some vineyards, cross over the motorway, and turn right on the N332 to Calpe. As you descend through more vineyards, flat-topped Oltá (Walk 3) and the rugged Bernia Ridge become prominent on the right, and the Peñón de Ifach (photograph pages 18-19) comes into view ahead. Take the left turn to Calpe Norte (130km ⊕), back to the Plaza Central, where the tour began (131km). If you feel like some exercise, why not follow the road signs to the Peñón de Ifach and walk through the tunnel and up to the top?

4 SOUTHERN VALLEYS AND WESTERN HIGHLANDS

Benidorm • Sella • Penáguila • Alcoi • Cocentaina • Bocairent • Cuevas de Canalobre • Benidorm

215km/133mi; 5 hours' driving; exit A from Benidorm (plan page 8)

On route: ⌷ at Penáguila, Font Roja, Cocentaina; Picnics (see **P** symbol and pages 10-15): 4, 18a, 18b-c, 19-22, 23a, 23b; Walks 4, 14, 17-23

From fertile valleys and heavily-wooded hillsides to desert wastes and stark peaks — this tour takes you through all manner of landscapes. Castles, caves and prehistoric paintings are just some of the features en route, and there are frequent opportunities to leave your car. Apart from exploring the interesting settlements it takes you through, we suggest several short strolls to the features of interest. To do and see everything would be too much for one day, so consider taking two days for this tour. Road renumbering is underway in the area; numbers on signposts often disagree with those on the roadside kilometre markers. Where differences exist at the time of writing we give both.

Take exit A from Benidorm, signposted to Alicante, and follow the signs to the Continente supermarket, where the tour starts. From the supermarket continue on the AP1735, making straight for the hills — the Cortina Ridge, with the notch of Campana standing out prominently behind it. Pass **Finestrat** (5km ✕), its houses perched precariously on a hillside, and circle clockwise to a minor crossroads, then turn left towards Sella on the AV1741. (A right turn would take you to parking for Walk 4 and **P**4.) This road climbs below Campana, affording good views of the 'shark's teeth' of El Realet. Benidorm is soon forgotten, as high-rise blocks and fancy villas give way to spectacular mountain peaks and grand old *fincas*.

At the T-junction (13km) turn right and head towards Penya Sella — a long flat ridge ending with three peaks on the right. Climb steeply above a *barranco* and terracing and go through **Sella** (17km ✕), noticing the contrast in vegetation on the slopes on either side of you — barren old almond terraces on the right-hand (sunny) side and dense woods on the left. Just as the road sweeps left (23km), a track rises to the right, signposted to the Remonte Aleman (German riding stables). Walk 14 which traverses the Penya Sella Ridge starts 5km up this track. Continuing on the A170 as it climbs steeply, ignore a left turn to Relleu. The antennas up on the right signal Aitana — Alicante's highest mountain. At a fork (27km) go left for 'Safari Aitana', 'Seguro', 'Penáguila' (A171 or AP1711). The road climbs high above the valleys, an eye-catching panorama spread before you, and then levels out before passing the Safari Park★ entrance (33km).

Now gradually descending the far side of the hill, you

pass through heavily-wooded terrain, which continues until the next valley opens out. On the far side of the rocky crag ahead are the remains of Penáguila Castle (Walk 22). Pass the gates of Casa Alta on the left (37km *P*22; Short walk 22). From this point the road winds down into **Penáguila** (41km ⬜️🚻🍴🚏) and then bears left towards Benifallím. On the next sharp right-hand bend, it is worth stopping to look behind you, where the the view of the castle and a natural rock arch (the Arco de Santa Llúcia) will long remain in your memory.

Continuing on the AP1711 pass the Mas de Pau *hostal* (43km 🏨) and adjacent *ermita* on the right (🚻). As you round another bend, **Benifallim** comes spectacularly into view, its castle on the left. Go through the village (45km) and follow the road (A161 or AP1711) towards Alcoi. It undulates through pleasant scenery to a T-junction at a bridge (52km 🍴), where you turn right on the N340 (🍴). In the background, the Barranc del Sinc slices through the rocky cliff face.

At the second set of traffic lights on the outskirts of **Alcoi★** (55km 🚻🏨🍴🚇⊕M📻), you can take an optional detour (signposted slip road on the right; 18km return) to the Santuario de la Font Roja★ (🚻🍴🚏△*P*21). This natural park, high in the mountains, is the setting for Walk 21 and well worth a visit. The main tour goes straight on at the lights, following the one-way system and signs to Valencia on the N340, winding all the way through Alcoi. This fascinating town, below the sheer cliffs of the Barranc del Sinc, has two centres, connected by huge bridges. You will surely want to delve into its history and explore its older quarters. Eventually you find yourself on the broad Avinguda l'Alameda, where you will cross a bridge over the Barranc del Sinc (58km). Just *before* the bridge, the supermarket Mercadona on the right is the starting point for Walk 18. But motorists can drive much closer to the fabulous setting shown on page 103 (*P*18a) by following the *walking notes* on page 101.

Continue over the bridge and, on leaving Alcoi, you will see Cocentaina Castle prominent ahead on its rocky pinnacle; Montcabrer (Walk 18), the main peak of the Sierra de Mariola rises majestically on the left. Drive through **Cocentaina** (63km 🚻🏨🍴🚇⊕🚏) and, at the traffic lights just before leaving the town, notice a road going left to the castle (⬜️) and the Sant Cristófol *zona recreativa* (🍴🚏*P*18b-c).

Some 6km from Cocentaina take the slip road signposted to Muro and Agres (C3311, A202). Turn left towards Agres and cross the pine-clad slopes of the Agres valley. After going under the railway (75km), climb gradually until Agres comes into view on the left. Above the village, clinging to the hillside, is the Ermita de la Mare de Deu (*P*19) which Walk 19 passes on its way to the refuge and the *cavas* (snow wells). Just after the 8km road marker, turn left (76km) and drive up to **Agres** (77km ✝▲✕). Turn left at the fork and wind up through the narrow streets of this interesting village. Continuing straight on at the crossroads (78km) would take you up Carrer Major to the church where Walk 19 starts, but the tour turns *right* into Carrer San Antonio. Pass Pensión Mariola and, at the end of the street (just at the end of the railings) turn sharp right and head back down to the main road. Turn left and continue west. As the road descends gently, look up to the left and see if you can spot Cava Gran, a circular stone building on top of the ridge; it is visited on Walk 19.

Drive through **Alfafara** (82km, now the A203) passing a couple of old *fincas* on the right, their terraced fields still well cultivated. Turn left at the T-junction (86km) signposted to Villena (CV81 or C3316), and prepare yourself for magnificent views of the old town of **Bocairent**★ (✝▲✕➘⊕M🚗), with its *ermita* high on a hill to the right. The town, shown opposite, is worth exploring: turn right (88km), following a sign for 'Centre Urba' and go over a bridge. Follow the one-way system and signs to the tourist office. You climb high into the village, to the large oval Plaza de la Ayuntamiento (89km). This houses the tourist office and museum. From here you can walk along a lane to the Covetes de los Moros★, described and illustrated on page 98. Short walk 17 will take you there, while the main walk (illustrated on the cover and page 97) goes along an old mule trail to Ontinyent. Both walks begin at the tourist office.

From the square, follow the signs 'Salida a Carretera' and, after crossing the bridge, turn right towards the petrol station (➘). Not far along the road (91km) turn left towards a signposted campsite. The road (VV2031) winds high above the Agres Valley on to a wooded plateau. Across the plateau the land opens out and several small farmhouses lie amongst the cultivated fields. After entering the woods once more, Mariola Castle appears ahead on a rocky peak. Just past the 9km road marker (100km Δ) you pass on the left the entrance to the commercial campsite

previously signposted. Beyond a small bridge, an unsurfaced road up to the left is signposted 'Font de Mariola
— Area Recreativa'. If you would like a break, turn up
here and park near the building which serves as a shelter
for campers and picnickers. This is Font Mariola's free
camping area, with picnic benches and a *font* ($\Delta \overline{R} P$20).
Walk 20, to Alt de la Cova, begins here and, just past the
benches, Short walk 20-2 leads up a track through pines
to Mariola Castle. Returning to the road, turn left and after
a few kilometres wind down across a narrow bridge.
Notice that the next road marker indicates only 5km; the
bridge marks a boundary, and the road (now the AP or
VV2031) is marked to the bridge from both directions!
Just continue ahead, ignoring these little idiosyncracies.
On reaching a crest, look ahead to the thickly-wooded
slopes: you can see the Font Roja sanctuary. To the left
and slightly lower down is Barchell Castle.

   Wind down into **Barchell** (109km) and, at the junction,
cross the bridge and turn right towards Banyeres (CV795
or AP3313). Within 300m pass a dirt road off to the left
which leads to Barchell Castle, a five minute walk away.
The road continues across the plain, through well-cultivated farmlands and past El Altet, another old *finca* on
the right. Turn left towards Ibi on the A200 (116km) and

Bocairent rises above its medieval bridge.

climb through fertile terraces, ignoring a right turn to Onil. This Castalla/Onil/Ibi area produces almost all the toys and dolls for the whole of Spain. From a crest, Ibi can be seen sprawled out in the valley below. The two hills to the north of the town used to bear castles, but nothing remains of them today. Instead there are two *ermitas*, one dedicated to Santa Lucia, the other to San Miguel.

Winding downhill you have a good view of the pointed peak of Maigmó ahead. As you approach the factory at the entrance to **Ibi** (125km ✝✗🖪), notice the two brick gate-posts on the left and a PR signpost. Walk 21 to Font Roja passes through here. Continue into town and, just before reaching the *ayuntamiento* (where Walk 21 begins), notice a street to the right: Calle Vicente Pascual. A little way along the street there is an interesting modern fountain — worth a quick visit. Set into its walls are ceramic tiles each bearing a picture — a shield or crest, a castle or *ermita*, all with some connection with Ibi.

Continue by turning left at the *ayuntamiento* and going straight on at the petrol station (🖪) on the A210. After passing large expanses of cultivated fields, turn right at the junction (135km) on to the N340 towards Jijona. This road crosses a high pass, and signs at the junction will tell you if it is open. But first, just after turning right, take a little road to the left signposted to **La Sarga** (AP1612). Drive about 0.5km through apple orchards to this small collection of houses, then leave them on the right: take the *camino rural* (136km), which soon sweeps to the left over the *barranco* and winds up to Mas de la Cova (*P*23b). Ahead in the rock face, just a short walk away, are caves where prehistoric paintings can be seen.

Return to the main road, turn left, and wind up to the **Puerto de la Carrasqueta**, a pass at 1020m/3350ft. Park at the *mirador* (144km 📷) and take in the surrounding views. Walk 23 to Pou del Surdo (*P*23a; photograph page 118) and the Carrasqueta Ridge starts here. Over the pass the road winds down through steep hairpins, with ample places to pull over and take in yet more stunning views (📷). On the downhill stretch (🖪 at 150 km and several ✗), you pass an *ermita* (155km) and soon see the distinctive split peak of Penya Roja which towers over Jijona.

A bypass is being built, but drive into **Jijona** (157km ✝▲✗🖪⊕M), the confectionery capital of Spain. Its situation in the centre of the almond-growing region determines its importance in the *turrón* (nougat) industry — it even has a museum of *turrón!* Unless you wish to explore the town, turn left (signposted to Alicante) and continue through the barren waste that the landscape around Jijona has become after years of drought. Occasional sproutings of vegetation in the dry river beds give evidence of some underground water — oases in what is otherwise essentially desert. About 3km south of Jijona (161km) turn left on the AV1821, signposted to Busot. This fairly rough, narrow road snakes downhill, crosses a bridge over a dry river bed and later, near the 3km marker, winds up to Toll del Carmello — where a pair of reservoirs comes as a surprise (169km).

Shortly after this, turn left uphill (170km) towards the Sierra de Cabezo de Oro. Situated at over 700m/2300ft, the **Cuevas de Canalobre**★ (175km **M**), with magnificent stalactites and stalagmites, are considered the most important in the Valencian region. They were used originally for cold storage, but in the Spanish Civil War they served as an arms depot. Rather incongruously, there is also an American Indian Museum alongside the caves. Even if you do not visit the caves, take a few minutes to admire the spectacular view (📷) over the valley.

From the caves return to the road, turn left (180km) and drive through **Busot** (182km). The notice 'Comparsa Els Contrabandistes' ('Smugglers' Group') above the door of a little house just before the *correos* has us wondering if this might have been an old smuggling town. At the main junction in the village, turn left for Aigües de Busot (not signposted until *after* you turn off) and climb through yet more hairpins round the rocky mountainside, before descending to the next junction (188km). Turn left to **Aigües de Busot** (191km ▲▲ ✕M). This is a spa town, busy at weekends. Follow the signs to Relleu, but after 2km turn right (193km) for Villajoyosa. This delightful narrow road undulates straight towards Campana, with the antennas of Aitana high on the left. At every turn and crest new beauties of nature come into focus; then the man-made Presa de Amadorio appears on the left (202km). Go through a tunnel, cross the wall of this huge reservoir and almost immediately overlook Villajoyosa.

Pass its rugby club on the left (205km) and, 50m further on, turn right at the T-junction. This road (A173) takes you through orange groves and into **Villajoyosa** (♠▲▲ ✕🎪⊕△). While still short of the centre, turn left (207km), following signposting for Benidorm. Skirt round the edge of the town, to a major junction (209km). Turn left (N332) and drive back into Benidorm (215km).

Alicante • Monforte del Cid • Castalla • Catí • Alicante

138km/86mi; 3 hours' driving. Exit A from Alicante (plan page 9). From elsewhere, join the tour at the A7 junction, just east of the N330.

On route: **⊼** at Novelda; Picnics (see **P** symbol and pages 10-15): 24, 25a, 25b, 26; Walks: 24, 25, 26

The province of Alicante played an important role in the history of the region during the seven or eight centuries of the Reconquest from the Moors. This role can be appreciated as you consider the vast number of castles which remain today, some in ruins, others well preserved or restored. One of the best known figures associated with the period must be El Cid, the legendary 11th-century mercenary considered at the time to be a national patriot. The town and the mountain named after him feature prominently on this tour.

From the roundabout at the railway station, head for the N330 to Madrid, driving towards the stark mounds of the Sierra de Fontcalent. The countryside is barren, parched following several years of drought. Continue past the A7 junction (4km ⊞) and after 1km join the N330 (⊞ 16km). On the far side of the Portichol Pass (⊞ 20km) take the slip road to **Monforte del Cid** (22km ⊡✝⊞). This town, said to be one of the two oldest settlements in the province, merits a visit. A church with a striking blue ceramic dome now stands on the old fortifications, its bell tower fashioned from one of the ancient defensive towers. The patio is paved, with flower beds and benches.

Follow signs for Madrid and Albacete to return to the N330, then turn off to **Novelda** (27km ⊡✝M). Its main products are table grapes and saffron, but its main attraction is its castle. After crossing the river bed, turn right (signposted to Elda), then left (same signposting). Then go left again, signposted to the Castillo de la Mola. More signs direct you towards the castle, which comes into sight after about 1km. There is ample parking space (34km). As you approached it was probably not the castle, but the impressive Santuario de la Magdalena which caught your eye. It is ornately arabesque and dates from 1912. The castle itself has been declared a national monument and is in the process of being restored. You will have noticed picnic benches (⊼) below the car park, but a better place to relax is at the top of the hill behind the sanctuary, where more benches afford a magnificent view over Aspe and Novelda.

Drive back into Novelda, turn left at the gardens, and then follow signs to Elda, to get back on the N330. Behind the pointed hill on your right, you have your first view of the impressive El Cid, its twin peaks joined by a long shallow plateau. This view improves as you drive through the still-barren terrain and take the exit for **Elda** (46km ⬚✝⛰✕🍴⊕M). This large town has a chequered past. In 1304 it passed from the kingdom of Castilla to that of Valencia and, after the expulsion of the Muslims in 1609, it was left deserted. Castellanos eventually repopulated the area, imposing their language (Spanish as we know it), despite the fact that all around, even one street away in Petrer, the people spoke Valenciano. As you drive through, follow signs to Sax. At the junction where Sax is *not* mentioned, turn right (signposted to Madrid).

After going under the railway line, notice the station off to the left; it is the starting point for Walk 24 which leads to the huge sand dune shown on page 123 and down a fascinating old trail along a watercourse. Continue on the west side of the Viñalopó River (AV4011) to **Sax** (59km ⬛). Its name derives from the Latin *saxum*, meaning large boulder. Turn right and drive through the town, round the right-hand side of the castle which sits on this 500m/1650ft-high boulder. It was built first by the Romans; reconstructed by the Arabs in the eighth century, it has one Roman and one Arabic tower. If you drive round the back, past the wooded slopes, you can park beside a gate and enter the grounds on foot. A short walk round the castle offers a good view of the surrounding countryside, cultivated with almonds and olives.

Leaving the castle behind, bear right across a bridge. At the roundabout (where you cross the railway and then the *autovia*), go straight on for Castalla (A211). On the left you will see the antennas on top of Penya Rossa and the flat-topped ridge of the Sierra del Fraile; to the right is the Sierra de la Argueña. Close to the 29km marker, alongside almond groves, pass a house either side of the road and then a track going to the left (67km). Walk 26 (*P*26) starts here and follows an old trail to the summit of Sierra del Fraile. Turning off to Castalla (70km), the first town you see ahead to the left is Onil, but then Castalla Castle appears on the right, the view becoming ever more magnificent as you draw nearer. Drive round its base to **Castalla** (76km ⬚✝✕🍴). The town's name derives from the Latin *castra alta* or high castle, for obvious reasons. It has not been completely restored, but is worth a visit. The town also has a baroque church dating from 1613, an *ermita* and an 18th-century convent. Go straight ahead at the traffic lights, passing the church on your right. As you leave the town, look for the bar-discotheque Triangulo on the left: you must turn right here into Calle

Azorín (marked by a red sign for 'Xorret de Catí' — an hotel). Similar signs later direct you left towards the crags of Despeñador and left again at a fork (78km); 300m to the *right* at this fork is the starting point for Walk 25 (*P*25a), a long, varied hike which takes in the summit of Despeñador. Keeping left, drive through extensive almond and olive groves towards the hills, then wind up steeply through pines until you are directly under Despeñador. The road takes you round to the left and up to a crest. The twin peaks of El Cid stand out ahead as you descend into the valley, where Xorret de Catí is visible below. Be careful here — you may encounter walkers on the road. At a junction (86km) follow the sign to Petrer and Elda. Pass the **Catí** hotel tennis courts and stop at the front entrance. You can avail yourself of the hotel facilities (✕🏔) or stretch your legs. Alternative walk 25-3 starts here, and walkers' signpost PR-V29 points the way to the Ermita de Catí (*P*25b).

From the hotel entrance, go back to the road and bear left, descending alongside a *barranco* on the right, into a dip where a walkers' signpost indicates the Pantanet Gorge off to the right (Walk 25). Continue up out of the dip for a view of the gorge. Pass Casa de Pantano and, at a junction (91km), turn right. (A left turn would take you to the foot of El Cid.) Continue the descent and, after a little more than 1km, look for a drystone wall on the left. This surrounds an old two-tier *era* (threshing floor), with its cylindrical millstone still in place. Shortly after this (93km) you see the beginnings of La Rambla dels Molins on the left, the watercourse on the route of Walks 24 and 25. Follow this past Restaurante Molino la Roja (✕ start of Short walk 24-1, *P*24), then drive high above the *rambla,* taking in its spectacular rock formations.

As you round a bend, Petrer Castle comes into sight. The tiny Carrer de las Casitas ('Street of the Little Houses') leading up to this Arabic castle is picturesque, and the castle itself is almost fully restored. Stop at the *mirador* (97km 📷) for a longer look; notice, too, the twin towns of Elda and Petrer and more views of El Cid. Wind downhill and turn right into **Petrer** (🚌🚻🏔✕🚍⊕). Go under the *autovía,* past Continente hypermarket, and turn left at the roundabout. Follow signposting for Alicante through the town, past a couple of pleasant garden areas (🚍 100km). Join the N330, pass the A7 junction (132km) and follow signs to the centre of Alicante. These will lead you back to the station roundabout (138km).

❀ Walking

While the car tours take you through spectacular country-side, it is really only when walking that you can fully appreciate the beauty of this landscape. From a car you would not notice the fish swimming contentedly in the clear and sparkling water of a mountain stream, the clump of orchids at the side of a path, the relentless call of the corn bunting or the sweet smell of rosemary. We hope that what you do see on your car tours will entice you to walk. *There are walks here for everyone to enjoy.*

As you will notice from any high vantage point, the mountains in the Costa Blanca region are criss-crossed by a myriad of tracks and paths. Some of these, used for centuries by farmers and shepherds, connect remote settlements and villages and provide access to *fincas*, *fonts* and fields. Others are more recent, sometimes the result of quarrying and forestry activities. The replacement of donkey and mule by tractor and trailer has resulted in many paths being widened into tracks and, in some cases, surfaced roads. Our walks follow footpaths wherever possible, but often tracks are unavoidable. However, these tracks are so little used that they should not spoil your enjoyment of the walks.

The area is well walked, and there are some classic routes, parts of which we have included. But we have, for example, rejected or adapted those which involve nothing more than a sheer slog to the summit of a mountain and back down again. In an attempt to tailor our walks specifically for users of *Landscapes* books, and taking into account the region's limited public transport service, we have tried to provide circular, rather than out-and-back walks. In order to make this possible we some-times include short stretches on asphalt roads. But these are always quiet country roads, generally free of traffic.

If you are walking on a Sunday or a *fiesta,* choose as remote a location as you can find. That is the day when Spaniards pack up their cars and head for the wide open spaces — to hunt, to gather wild mushrooms, to collect water from mountain *fonts*, to picnic or simply to enjoy a drive. Roads will be busy, and picnic sites with benches and car access could well be chock-a-block.

Unless you are doing one of the walks close to the

39

tourist beat, the accepted greeting for other walkers or for farmers is the Valenciano *Bon día*, rather than the Spanish *Buenos días*. It will always elicit a hearty response.

It is important that all walkers read and *heed* the country code on pages 10-11.

Grading and timing

When **grading** each walk, we have tried to describe the effort required, the state of the paths, and the ease of navigation. You need not be an expert or even a habitual walker to tackle most of our walks, but a reasonable level of fitness and stamina, as well as some mountain 'sense', is assumed. *Be sure to read through the whole description of a walk before setting out,* so that you know *exactly* what to expect and what to take with you. ***If the main walk looks too strenuous for you,*** see if there are any short or alternative versions which are less demanding. You need look no further than the picnic suggestions on pages 10-15 to find a wide selection of ***very easy walks.***

Despite being in our fifties, *we tend to walk faster than most,* except perhaps on tricky descents. Please compare your pace with ours on one or two short walks, *before* setting out on a long hike. You may have to adjust our timings to suit your own pace — remember this when planning bus or train connections. We give **frequent time checks.** They are ***not*** meant to be followed minute-by-minute throughout the walk, but to indicate the easily-monitored ***time difference*** between various points. Check our notes frequently, to avoid missing turn-offs or landmarks. Our **overall timings** do not include any stops. Allow time for lunch, photography, bird-watching and botanising. Take account of the weather, too. Hot sun, driving rain and strong winds can affect your rate of progress.

Waymarking and maps

Some of the tourist offices will, if pressed, provide a pamphlet (normally in Spanish) about walks in their area. *But beware!* These are pictorial and very pretty, but usually devoid of description and detail. At best you will find them almost impossible to follow; at worst they could get you completely lost and into some dangerous terrain.

We are confident that you will find the instructions for walks in this book both clear and comprehensive. Some of the paths are not **waymarked** at all. Others have been marked by local walking groups. You will see the red and white striped waymarks of the GR ('Gran Recorrido') long distance footpaths and the yellow and white stripes of the

PR ('Pequeño Recorrido') short distance walks. Elsewhere there are coloured dots, or arrows and cairns — or a combination of all of these. Our walks sometimes coincide with marked routes but seldom follow them all the way — *so don't get carried away by the markings; read our instructions.*

The **maps** in this book have been updated from Spanish military surveys (1970s/1980s); they were correct at press date but, as more of the countryside is exploited, new tracks or roads are likely to appear. All the paths and tracks of our walks are marked in green, and *we would advise you to stick to these.* Beware of Spanish maps; they often place tracks or paths, and even roads, in the wrong place (or not at all!); conversely, they sometimes include tracks or trails which do not exist.

Where to stay

If you taking a package holiday you will undoubtedly find yourself situated in one of the **coastal towns**. If travelling independently and keen to walk, you might prefer to stay **in the mountains**. You will not find top-class hotels, but there are a few *pensiones* and *hostales* (some English-run). Even in the smallest villages there may be someone willing to offer you basic hospitality. Tourist offices provide a list of accommodation, but it is by no means complete — village bars are a better source of advice. There are **campsites** in Vall d'Alcalá (good facilities, uninspiring site), Vall d'Ebo (basic but grassy, with plenty of trees), Font Mariola (both a huge commercial site, with all facilities, and, less than 1km away, a much more attractive, free municipal site, with a *font*) and Font Roja (reasonable facilities and no charge).

Weather

With care, you can walk comfortably in this region all year round — as long as you **heed the weather signs and carry appropriate equipment**. The best time to walk is undoubtedly spring, when the hillsides are carpeted with a huge variety of colourful and delicate flowers and herbs — providing a feast for butterflies and birds and a great spectacle for walkers. But the limestone rock and the nature of the climate ensures that you will find some flowers in bloom in the mountains at any time of year.

There can be **frost** in the mountains in winter with **snow** on the highest peaks and **strong winds** in exposed areas may make it feel very cold sometimes. February and November can be quite wet; **heavy storms**, which cause damage to tracks and paths, often occur in September and early October. Such storms, though not usually very long-lasting, can be quite unexpected and frighteningly fierce, so make sure you are prepared. The strength of the **sun** should not be ignored at any time of the year, and it can be blisteringly hot from May to October.

What to take

The mountains of the Costa Blanca are unlikely to present the sort of extreme weather conditions that might be encountered at home but, nevertheless, you should equip yourself for all eventualities. The sun can be strong at any time of the year, so **suncream, sunhat and long-sleeved shirt** should always be taken with you on walks. According to the season and prevailing weather conditions, you must judge what **extra items of clothing** you might need. Storms *can* occur in summer, and even on a bright sunny day it can be very chilly at high altitude — so take **warm and waterproof clothing** on mountain walks. The whole area tends to be very rocky underfoot and **stout, thick-soled shoes, preferably with ankle support, are a must** for all but one or two of the walks. Unless you are walking in extremely bad weather you should not require heavy boots, but for comfort we certainly recommend lightweight hiking boots or shoes. Paths and tracks can be very muddy for a day or so after heavy rain, with the clay-like soil clinging to your boots. The other essential is **water**. Bottled water is widely available. There are *fonts* on a few of the walks but in summer months you are quite likely to find they are dry. For all longer walks you should take a **picnic lunch**.

For each walk, we specify any additional items you will require. We have sometimes included **compass** directions as extra confirmation of the route to take. Although all the walks can be followed without a compass it would be foolish to tackle any of the high mountain ones without one, since mist or cloud can soon obliterate landmarks and lead to disorientation.

For **emergencies** it is always wise to carry a **first-aid kit,** some high energy food, extra water, a couple of large black plastic bags, whistle, compass, torch and some warm clothing.

Nuisances

Dogs might be encountered as you pass close to farms, but they are generally chained up or fenced in. The sudden noise of their barking as they sense an alien presence can give you a fright, but they should present no threat. You are more likely to come across loose dogs on the outskirts of towns and villages. They bound out of a gateway straight towards you and refuse to let you pass. In this situation we stand still and shout until someone appears and calls the dog off. Should you wish to invest in an ultrasonic dog deterrent, write to Dazer UK, Freepost, London SW11 6BR.

It is unlikely that you will have a problem with either **snakes** or **scorpions**, but you should be aware of the possibility — greater if you are just a couple of walkers proceeding quietly. In warm weather we see snakes quite regularly, usually slithering out of our way at the side of a path, disturbed by our approach. The only poisonous snake is a viper with a triangular yellowish head and a zigzag line down its spine. A bite from one of these needs urgent medical attention. Scorpion stings should also be treated quickly. But you will avoid problems if you are careful: keep to the path, do not disturb rocks or stones, and think twice before sitting on a drystone wall.

Organisation of the walks

The area covered by this guide is bounded by the coast in the east, the Sierra de Benicadell in the north, the Sierras of Mariola and Maigmó in the west, and the city of Alicante in the south. This inverted triangle includes a very complex topography, with over 35 named sierras, both rugged and gentle, interspersed by a large number of picturesque valleys. This complexity makes for fascinating and varied walking, but makes it difficult to group the walks in a simple way.

We have chosen to split the walks into six groups, categorised by the coastal strip in the east, the sierras forming the western border of the area, and those based around groups of valleys going roughly west to east:

Walks 1-5: Coastal strip from Denia to Benidorm
Walks 6-9: Serpis and Gallinera valleys
Walks 10-12: Laguart and Jalón valleys
Walks 13-16: Guadalest, Algar and Sella valleys
Walks 17-22: Alcoi area
Walks 23-26: Sierras of Carrasqueta and Maigmó

You will probably start with walks closest to where you are based, but all are quite accessible from any of the coastal resorts. You'll find an overview of the walk areas on the fold-out touring map, and a quick flip through the book will reveal at least one photograph for each walk. Each description begins with planning information: times and distances, grade, equipment and how to get there. For some of the main walks we suggest possible alternatives and give a short version wherever feasible. Before the detailed description of the route there is a general introduction to give you a 'feel' for the landscape. The 1:50,000 maps have been specially annotated for use with the text, and feature the following symbols:

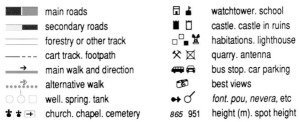

▬▬▬	main roads	🏠 🔔	watchtower. school
▬▬	secondary roads	■ ☐	castle. castle in ruins
═══	forestry or other track	□ ■ ⚓	habitations. lighthouse
─ ─ ─	cart track. footpath	✕ ⊠	quarry. antenna
→	main walk and direction	🚐 🚌	bus stop. car parking
••••⇒•••	alternative walk	📷	best views
○ ○ ☐	well. spring. tank	↔ ♂	font. *pou, nevera, etc*
✝ ✝ ⊞	church. chapel. cemetery	*865 951*	height (m). spot height

Finally, we would like to **highlight five walks** which will give you a good cross-section of the terrain and landscape. **Walk 1** takes you to a mountain summit; **Walk 6** leads along a beautiful river valley and up to a castle; **Walk 10** traverses amazing Mozarabic trails from the Middle Ages; **Walk 13** follows some gentle mountain valleys under the highest mountain in Alicante province; and **Walk 19** visits 17th-century 'snow wells' (*cavas*) on a high mountain ridge.

Walk 1: On the descent from Montgó, we meet some walkers climbing to the summit. Jávea lies below. Most of the paths on this walk are rocky and, while wide enough to be comfortable, they still demand care and attention.

1 MONTGO

See also plan page 9 and photographs opposite and page 11

Distance: 13km/8mi; 5h48min

Grade: quite strenuous, with a climb and descent of 640m/2100ft on good, but rocky paths. You must be surefooted and have a head for heights. Navigation is straightforward throughout. Avoid windy days.

Equipment: see page 42; also walking boots with ankle support, compass, extra water in summer

How to get there and return: 🚌 to/from Montgó Natural Park (see Car tour 1 at the 93km-point); also by taxi or on foot from Denia railway station (add 30min each way if walking; see plan page 9).

Short walk: Cova de l'Aigua. 3.5km/2.2mi; 1h. Easy. Equipment as page 42. Access/return as main walk. Follow the main walk to the 19min-point and turn left. A few minutes later take the marked path on the right to the Cova de l'Aigua. Return the same way.

Alternative walk: Cova de l'Aigua and Cova del Camell. 11km/6.8mi; 3h30min. Easy. Equipment as page 42. Access/return as main walk. Follow the short walk to the Cova de l'Aigua, but turn right when you come back down to the Camí de la Colonia (43min). Continue as far as the Cova del Camell (1h55min) and return the same way.

The Parque Natural del Montgó takes its name from the forbidding-looking mountain shown on page 11 which forms the backdrop to the resorts of Denia and Jávea. This walk ascends its northeast face, descends south towards Jávea, then skirts the foot of the mountain on an old trail.

Start out at the entrance to the Parque Natural: take the track behind the chain barrier. It zigzags up the lower slopes to an old trail, the Camí de la Colonia (**19min**), which contours round the foot of Montgó. Turn right (at the end of the walk you will come in here from the left, and *the Short and Alternative walks turn left now*). The humidity on this face of the mountain encourages the growth of lush ferns, but has not prevented fires destroying or damaging many of the pines. The trail peters out into a footpath (**31min**) and begins to climb ... more steeply as it approaches the face of the sheer cliff. A short level stretch under the cliff offers a brief respite (**56min**), just before you meet another narrow path coming up from the Cova de l'Aigua.

Fork right here (**1h03min**) and head uphill again on a steep, rocky path lined with wild flowers. Just before a crest (**1h28min**) a path comes in from the right, by a cairn. This is one of the other routes up the mountain, via the Penya del Águila, and if you are very lucky you may see the eagles *(águilas)* after which the Penya is named.

From the crest head left on an obvious path lined with lavender and rosemary. Ahead, a large cross marks a peak, but this is *not* the summit. On rounding a bend (**2h05min**) the true summit, also marked with a cross, comes into view. Your path, sometimes narrow and exposed, snakes along to a lone pine and a cave, and then up to the top of Montgó (753m/2470ft; **2h45min**). Inland the sierras unfold layer by layer; along the coast, you can see as far as Gandía to the north and Calpe to the south. On a clear day Ibiza is visible on the eastern horizon.

Standing with the cross between you and the sea, look inland: your descent path lies over to the left, within five metres of the cross, heading a little east of south. The first section is a bit of a scramble down the rocky slope; for the easiest route, follow the clear red paint marks. The scramble ends (**3h12min**) and you join the well-built path shown on page 44, which zigzags all the way down the middle slopes. As you get lower, look down and locate your goal: a clear, wide path, originating in a *barranco* and winding round the foot of the mountain to the left.

Just after a short uphill section, Jávea comes into view ahead. Ignore all the steep short-cut paths through the thickening vegetation, so as not to miss the yellow way-marks on the left (**4h**) which indicate your route to Denia. They lead you over the rocks and along the right bank of a *barranco,* to a path from where the holding wall of the wide path you saw from above is visible. Descend into the *barranco,* passing the Cova del Camell (**4h13min**).

Cross the *barranco* and climb to the path above, the Camí de la Colonia. It is flat, beautifully constructed and provides ever-changing views over the coast. After passing an old kiln and a cistern, you will meet another, rather dauntingly steep, route up to the summit. Beyond two more cisterns and a ruined house, you reach the steep path up to the Cova de l'Aigua (signposted; **5h25min**) — an impressive natural cavity with a permanent spring. It is no longer exploited but, in the past, it provided much of Denia's water. (Allow 20min return, if you have energy for this detour.) Continue on the Camí to the junction with your outward track (**5h30min**). Turn right downhill, back to the park entrance (**5h48min**).

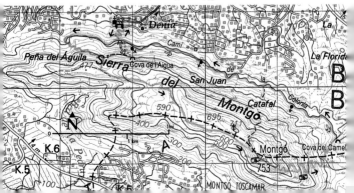

2 SHORT WALKS AROUND JAVEA

Equipment for all walks: see page 42; also swimming gear for Walks 2c-e. Trainers should suffice as footwear.

Distance, grade, access: see individual walks.

a   Cap de San Antonio. 4km/2.5mi; 1h34min. Easy. By 🚗 or on foot to the port at the northern end of Jávea. See text below.

b   Los Molinos. 5km/3mi; 1h28min (with detour 7km/4.3mi; 2h24min). The main walk is an easy stroll; the optional detour is very steep and strenuous and requires great care. 🚗 to the *zona recreativa* on the Cap de San Antonio road (see Car tour 1 from about 76km). Ample parking and 🍴, water taps; pleasantly set amidst pines. See text page 48.

c   Cabo San Martín. 2km/1.2mi; 56min. Easy. 🚗 to the Cruz del Portichol, a stone cross on the AV1331 (the 55km-point on Car tour 1). Pick up text on page 49. **See photograph page 11.**

d   Playa Portichol. 3km/1.9mi; 1h09min. Easy, except for the climb on the road on the return section. This is steep but, taken slowly, worthwhile (or it can be avoided by returning from the *playa* by the outward route). Access as for (c) above. See text page 50.

e   Granadella. 3km/1.9mi; 1h09min. Strenuous climb and descent, but the paths are good. 🚗 as for (c) above, but continue for about 2km past the cross, then turn right for Granadella: 4km down this road (AV1332) you reach the Playa de Granadella, a small secluded cove sheltered by high cliffs. Park at the beach (busy in the season). See text page 51.

These five short walks provide a good cross-section of coastal scenery in this delightful area. The secluded coves, rugged headlands and old windmills capture the beauty of the landscape around Jávea.

Start Walk a by following the coast road past the port and the Red Cross building. Just beyond the Club Naútico, when the road ends (**6min**), go up some concrete steps to the left. These give way to a narrow rocky path, marked in red, which snakes up the hillside. At a fork, go left, along the left-hand side of a *barranco*. Cross this stream bed (**19min**) and turn right along its far bank, heading east towards Cap de San Antonio. Here you lose the way-marking. At **25min** ignore a path downhill to the right and continue gently climbing. In spring the scent of rosemary and pine mingle tantalisingly, and in autumn the slopes are clad with heather. The clear path contours round the slopes, circles the head of another *barranco* (**34min**) and eventually forks (**46min**). The right fork goes to the lighthouse on the headland at Cap de San Antonio. Take the left fork, which leads you up to a car park and *mirador* (📷) with a water tap on the main Cap de San Antonio road (**49min**). From here you have a fantastic view down to Jávea. Cap de San Antonio is 200m away to the right. To the left, eight minutes' walk away, is a *zona recreativa* where you could link up with the start of Walk 2b. Otherwise, retrace your steps back to the port (**1h34min**).

Start Walk b on the wide track which heads off to the left just before the benches. Walk alongside the boundary wall of a house; ignore a track going left (**2min**). At a junction (**9min**) fork right. At **20min** you reach a T-junction with an old abandoned *cuartel* (military barracks) just off to the left. Turn left*, pass the *cuartel* and some villas, and reach the main Cap de San Antonio road (**25min**). Cross the road and walk up Camí del Monastir, which follows the boundary walls of an imposing *santuario*. This narrow poplar-lined road is asphalted at first but soon becomes unsurfaced. As it sweeps left (you will return this way later) go straight ahead (**31min**) and you will see the first windmill *(molino)* at the top of the crest just in front of you.

More mills are lined up along the crest, most to the right, one to the left — twelve in all. First visit the mills to the right. Take the path going up to the first mill and continue along past the others, some of which are now privately owned and which you skirt round on a path on the Jávea side of the cliff. A narrow asphalt road (**41min**) takes you the remaining few metres to the path up to the last three in this line of mills (**46min**), from where views are spectacular (**P**2b; photograph page 50).

Retrace your steps to the point where you reached the crest (**55min**). The path which runs downward below the mills winds its way into Jávea, but you turn left, back towards the *santuario*. After about 100m/yds turn right on the unsurfaced road going towards the sea, then take a track going off right through some large metal gates (**1h**). This leads past a stone cross to the twelfth mill. The path then meanders down a few terraces and meets a track which runs along the top of a deep *barranco*. You want to be on the other side, so turn left and follow the track round the top of the *barranco*. At **1h03min** reach the dirt road you left a few minutes ago and turn right. Notice the game bird breeding aviary nearby on the left — usually full of partridge — and turn left on the asphalted Calle Cuesta de San Antonio (a right turn here leads down into

---

*If you are surefooted and agile, you can take a 1h detour: turn *right* here. After five minutes, on a left-hand bend (just after a wall), take a path off to the right, past a *font* and a little water tank. After crossing an open area it descends very steeply down rocky slopes to a large cave, the Cova Tallada, almost at sea level. Retrace your steps to the junction.

Jávea port). Cross the main Cap de San Antonio road (**1h13min**), go straight ahead and, after 100m/yds, turn right on a narrow track. This joins your outward track (**1h16min**) and takes you back to the *zona recreativa* (**1h28min**).

Start Walk c by looking out from the cross: you will see the island of Portichol to the right and the rocky headland of Cabo San Martín to the left. Directly below, a path winds downhill and then runs alongside some old grassy terraces, beyond which there are pines (**P**2c). Take the path which leads down from the cross, but turn left at a junction after only about 30m/yds (Walk 2d goes straight on here). Pass the terraces. The path takes you to the edge of the cliff, then bears left along the southern side of the

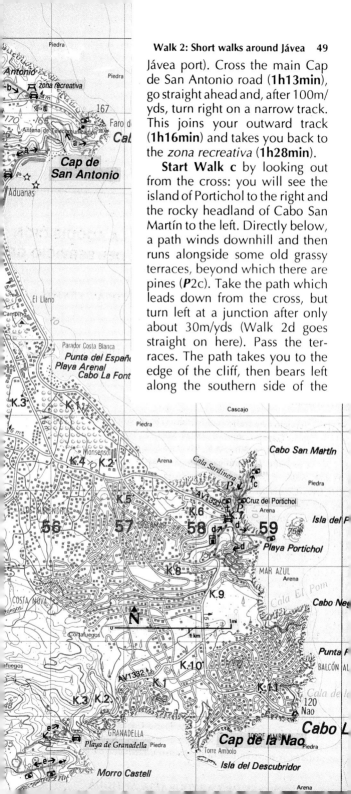

Los Molinos at Jávea (Picnic 2b and Walk 2b). They were positioned to catch the best of the winds, vital for the grinding of the grain grown long ago on the terraces. It is over a hundred years since they were last in use, but only one of them is a complete ruin. The towers of the rest remain solid although they have all lost their cones and sails.

headland. At **9min** the view of Montgó looming ahead is probably the finest you will ever have of that forbidding mountain (shown on page 11). Ignore a path left to Cala Sardinera and continue to the trig point on Cabo San Martín (**19min**). If it is not windy, and you feel brave, you can go a little further out on the rocky promontory. We prefer just to admire the views, before turning round and taking the path along the northern side of the headland, overlooking Cala Sardinera.

Just after rejoining your outward path, turn right on a path which takes you above the Cala. This path is very eroded — *don't* be tempted to make your way down any of the shortcuts. Wait till you reach the concrete steps (**45min**) which will take you safely down (**P**2c), perhaps for a swim, before returning up the steps and continuing along the path back up to the cross (**56min**).

Start Walk d from the cross, as Walk c, but go straight ahead at the junction 30m/yds downhill. This pleasant path passes below a drystone wall, then takes you through low pines. You are likely to see crag martins soaring and diving around the cliffs. In **8min** pass a path to the right (you will descend this path later). Continue straight on to the end of the headland, overlooking the Isla del Portichol (**13min**). As you round the cliff to the right, views open up. To the left is Cabo San Martín, with Cap de San Antonio beyond it. Ahead, Playa Portichol comes into view, overlooked by a restaurant and villas stretching far up the hillside. Return to the main path off the headland and turn left (**18min**) on the path you passed earlier. It is badly eroded but takes you down to the pebbly beach (**23min**) — another good spot for a swim.

To return, take the road which goes steeply up and out of the *playa,* past elaborate villas with huge expanses of drystone wall enclosing their different levels. Turn right at the junction signposted to Jávea (**41min**) and right again (**45min**) when you reach the main Cap de la Nao road. Almost immediately turn right once more into Carrer de la Torre, a narrow road which soon becomes a track and then dwindles into a path. When it appears that you are entering someone's back garden (**54min**), just go ahead and take the stone steps which go up to the left as you pass the house. These lead to another house which has an old sixteenth-century *torre*, or watchtower, within its boundary. Go along the top terrace to the left, to get a better view of this solid and well-preserved old building. To continue, go back down the steps and turn left (**1h 03min**). You are soon on a narrow road which leads back to Cruz del Portichol (**1h09min**).

Start Walk e at the car park: go back a few metres and walk away from the beach along a dry river bed which runs below the road. Join the road again and then take a left turn towards the cliffs (**3min**). Almost immediately, at a junction, fork left up a steep concreted road marked 'Camino Particular'; it is waymarked with red paint dots. Wind uphill, ignoring tracks left and right. The road peters out into a track (**15min**). Just after another track goes off to a large house on the right (**18min**), climb the well-waymarked path up the embankment on your right.

This path takes you through pine, gorse, rosemary and thyme, and emerges on a crest (**29min**). Waymarking ceases at this point. Turn left on the track along the ridge, enjoying sea views on both sides — Montgó towering over Cap de San Antonio to the left and, to the right, Cap de Moraira with the Peñón de Ifach behind it. At **35min** the track goes straight ahead to a water deposit and shallow concrete reservoir; another track leads off right to the edge of the cliff, from where views are spectacular. You will probably disturb some of the partridge which inhabit the open ground around here and appear to be almost tame. Take some time to explore this area, then retrace your steps to the crest and back down the path to the right (**45min**). Back on the concrete road, descend steeply to the Playa de Granadella (**1h09min**).

3 VUELTA DE OLTA (OLTA CIRCUIT)

Distance: 11km/6.8mi; 3h20min   **See also photograph pages 18-19**

Grade: moderate, with climbs and corresponding descents of about 360m/1180ft overall. Mostly on easy tracks, but surefootedness is essential on a few short sections. The initial climb to the circuit track is steep. Navigation is straightforward. The circuit track is waymarked with yellow rings and some red dots — look for them at junctions. Don't be confused by yellow arrows pointing in both directions (for the circuit).

Equipment: see page 42

How to get there and return: 🚌 or 🚊 to Calpe station

This clockwise walk around the Oltá peaks undulates roughly between the 300m and 400m contours. Each time you emerge from the shade of fragrant pine trees you will have spectacular views over Calpe and the coastline or towards the serrated ridges of surrounding sierras.

Start out by crossing the railway lines just beyond the station and going up the asphalt road for about 100m/yds. Then take the second road on the left. After about 50m/yds, fork right, heading towards Oltá. Pass a telephone box on your left, then fork right again. The asphalt ends (**8min**), and a forestry road continues. At **15min** fork right once more and, just after, ignore a track coming in from the right. Ignore another track coming in from the right (**20min**). At a three-way junction, where there are fine views ahead to the Sierra de Toix (**24min**), go straight on. Ignore a track to the left (**31min**); you reach the circuit track (**33min**); directly in front of it are the ruins of a house.

Turn left; the crags of Oltá's southern summit now rise steeply above you, as you climb gradually for about 100m/yds. After a sweeping right-hand bend, take the next track to the left. You are now on level ground again and Calpe is spread out before you, from its southern harbour under the Morro de Toix to the Peñón de Ifach guarding its northern harbour.

Pass a ruined *finca* on your left (**40min**) and continue until the track drops a few metres/yards before petering out (**44min**). The next section is a scramble up to the right, climbing several terraces. Look for the yellow paint rings on the rocks to confirm your route, *and watch your step.* As you climb, the panorama now includes the Mascarat Gorge with its three tunnels overlooked by the ruins of Calpe Castle. Beyond the castle, the Sierra Helada shelters Benidorm from the sea. After about 100m/yds the path levels out and contours around the southwestern flank of Oltá. It is eroded in places and for about ten minutes the terrain is barren and fire-scarred.

Throughout the traverse of this western flank the peaks

of the Sierra Bernia dominate the skyline to the west, more of it coming into view with every step you take. Watch as the whole length of this magnificent ridge, shown below, opens out before you. At **58min**, where there are some tall pines, the original track has been washed away by storms, and a short scrambling detour must be made up to the right (clearly marked). You cross a section of loose rocks and reach some terraces after about 100m/yds. Notice the *madroños* (wild strawberry bushes) on the terraces; the fruits, present at the end of summer and beginning of autumn, are edible but not particularly tasty. More inviting is the sweet-smelling thyme which seems to be particularly plentiful. A minute later, near the top of the terraces and just before a small house, you come to a good path where you must turn down left.

Reach a track (**1h08min**), turn right and look ahead to the left for your next objective, a ruined house perched on the hillside about 500m/0.3mi away. Pass it (**1h15min**), then ignore a track coming in from the left. Continue past an old gabbro quarry, evidenced by the grey rocks strewn around. Ignore another track coming in from the left at the quarry, but take note of the 'needles' below Oltá's north summit and another abandoned house. At a T-junction (**1h29min**) turn sharp right to reach the house (**1h38min**), from where the photograph below was taken.

Now, as you climb steeply, Oltá's northern summit (591m/1940ft) towers above you. Pass below the 'needles' and an interesting rock formation, ignoring firebreak tracks off to the right. The track descends to meet another track at a T-junction (**1h49min**). Turn right here and head for yet another ruined house situated between the north

Bernia Ridge, from the house passed at 1h38min into the walk

summit and Little Oltá (418m). The flat area in front of the house is a good place to take a break, but your ongoing path is about 150m/yds *before* the house: look to your left for a large boulder with red waymarks. Take the narrow downhill path beside the boulder, descending to a plateau with tall pines (**2h03min**). Cross the plateau diagonally, to the track ahead. Turn right downhill on the track, straight towards the Peñón de Ifach. Ignore a zigzag track to the left (which your track shortly rejoins) and pass a few houses and cultivated terraces. After the first house on the left, the track becomes a narrow asphalt road and winds past more houses. Just opposite Casa d'Agostino (**2h18min**) climb a narrow, badly-surfaced road uphill to the right. As you pass between old metal gateposts and curl up towards Little Oltá, ignore side tracks. At **2h24min** go straight ahead past Casa Mikadi, ignoring a track to the right. Some 100m/yds further on, the road sweeps to the left past another villa; here keep straight ahead on a mainly level track. At times narrowing to a footpath (and with one section of gentle rocky ascent), the track winds through pines, often alive with the twittering of coal tits and long tailed tits. You enjoy a constantly-changing view of the coast, from the Cap de Moraira to Calpe, with the Peñón de Ifach and Calpe Salinas dominating the scene (photograph pages 18-19). At a junction (**2h34min**) turn right on a forestry road marked with the yellow rings. Ignore two tracks off left to a house and then another one beckoning you up the mountain on your right.

The track reduces to a path once more (**2h44min**), as it curls right around a water deposit. The path leads you to a forestry road, and soon the southern summit of Oltá (539m) appears ahead of you. At the junction (**2h54min**) your circuit is complete: go straight ahead, retracing your outward route back to Calpe station (**3h20min**).

4 SIERRA DE CORTINA

Distance: 7km/4.3mi; 2h   **Grade:** easy ascent/descent of 260m/850ft
Equipment: see page 42

How to get there and return: 🚗 car or taxi from Benidorm. Take the C3318 going north (exit B) and turn left after about 3km on the Finestrat road (AV1741). Shortly before the 4km marker fork left for 'Rancho Puig Campana' (a huge restaurant); park in the car park. Ask the taxi driver to return for you, or telephone a taxi from the restaurant.

Short walk: Northeast ridge. 2km/1.2mi; 35min. Grade, equipment, access as above. Follow the main walk to the saddle, but turn left and use the notes from the 1h34min point to the end of the walk.

This low-level ridge walk, close to Benidorm, affords magnificent views along the coast from Alicante to Calpe and inland to the imposing sierras.

Start out by climbing the wide track to the left of the restaurant; ignore all side tracks. After only **10min** you are at the saddle on top of the Cortina Ridge (*P*4). Looking out to the coast, you will see the Sierra Helada stretching north from Benidorm (photograph below) and, a little further on, the Peñón de Ifach at Calpe. Inland to the north is the Sierra Bernia, while Puig Campana and its sister peak, Ponoch, dominate the view to the west.

You will explore the whole ridge — first to the southwest, then to the northeast. Turn right *(left for the Short walk)* and follow the track (later a path), as it steadily ascends a succession of rises over the different peaks on the southwest side. If you don't feel the need to conquer each one, take the side paths which bypass the highest points. From the last peak (**48min**) you have a fine view west to Finestrat and down the valley beyond it to Sella. Continue to the end of the ridge (**51min**) before returning to the saddle, this time enjoying the views to the north (**1h34min**).

Sierra Helada from Cortina Ridge

From here climb up to the most northerly peak of the ridge (**1h46min**), to gain a different perspective of Campana and another good view of the Sierra Bernia. Return to the saddle and turn right down to the Rancho (**2h**).

5 SIERRA HELADA: PUNTA DE PINET • ALBIR

Distance: 10km/6.2mi; 4h   **See also town plan page 8**

Grade: strenuous, with steep ascents and corresponding descents of 625m/2050ft overall. You must be surefooted and have a head for heights. Paths are often eroded and sometimes uncomfortably close to the edge of the sheer cliffs (**danger of vertigo**). Navigation is straightforward.

Equipment: see page 42; also proper walking boots or shoes, compass, extra water in summer

How to get there: 🚌 taxi, car or on foot to Restaurante Pergola in Calle Hamburgo at the end of Benidorm's Playa Levante. This is on the bend just as the road rounds the headland at Punta de Pinet. Parking could be difficult in the summer months.

To return: 🚌 from Albir; alight at Rincón de l'Oix (if you parked your car at Punta de Pinet) or in the centre of Benidorm.

Short walks (access as main walk; equipment as page 42)

1 Benidorm — El Mendivil — Benidorm. 4km/2.5mi; 1h50min. Fairly strenuous climb/descent of 330m/1080ft, but no danger of vertigo. Follow the main walk for 56min, then return the same way.

2 Benidorm — La Torre — Benidorm. 3km/1.9mi; 1h15min. Easy. Go through the gap in the blue railings at Playa Levante ('Entrada a la Playa' is painted on the rocks), and head down to the cove below. Take the path round to the headland above the next cove, Cala Ti Ximo. From here follow an asphalt road to the next headland, then continue on a footpath to the Punta de la Escaleta (*P5*). Now climb a path up to another asphalt road and follow it to the ruins of La Torre, a 17th-century watchtower (35min) with a superb outlook to the cliffs of the Sierra Helada. To return, either retrace your steps or follow the asphalt road.

Despite its proximity to Benidorm, the Sierra Helada is no mean mountain and must be treated with respect. From the landward side its undulating silhouette appears benign, but from the sea its sheer, stepped cliffs present a formidable picture. This exhilarating hike follows the cliff edge, with fantastic views.

Start out at the blue railings overlooking the beach and small cove: walk up the asphalt road. Turn left past the Castell del Mar apartments (**4min**), then turn right up the hill (**8min**). Ignore a road going off left after a few metres/yards. As you round a bend, notice the hill to the left of the Radio Benidorm antennas — this is your first objective. It used to bear a large wooden cross, but this has fallen over. A steep, eroded short-cut path goes up to the left (**23min**), but we continue along the road. Pass the antennas (**28min**) and, just before coming level with the summit, take the path up right to the summit (**31min**), where you can catch your breath while enjoying the views.

From here on the walk is waymarked in red, sometimes indistinctly, sometimes

lavishly, but there are occasions when it disappears for a while. Basically, just progress along the ridge, heading generally northeast, alternately climbing to the cliff tops and then dropping steeply to cross the gullies.

Either take the narrow path going down to the right just past the cross, or continue on the main path; the two paths rejoin a few metres below. Descend to a fork and bear left above a *barranco* on a well-trodden rocky path. It takes you round the head of the *barranco* (**38min**) and starts climbing to the top of the first cliff, called El Mendivil. This spot, popular with retired expatriates and locals alike, is marked with a small cairn (**56min**; 338m/ 1100ft). *Short walk 1 turns back here.*

From here the walk makes for the end of the sierra, where the antenna of the relay station is visible. But there are a lot of ups and downs to negotiate before you reach it. From the myriad of small paths round the cairn, take the most obvious one along the cliff top (the only way-marked route). When you come to the end of the level section, take the rough, rocky path waymarked in red and yellow; it descends into a gully, close to the edge of the cliff. Cross the gully (**1h08min**) and, having lost about 50m/165ft of altitude, you must now regain it. Continue within a few metres/ yards of the cliff edge to the next peak. Cairns supplement the red dots as you head down into the next,

The Sierra Helada, from the top of the first gully. Five major gullies are crossed before reaching the relay station on the highest point in the range (438m/ 1440ft).

shallower gully. As you cross it (**1h25min**), you can see two routes up to the next peak. Make your choice of path and reach the top at **1h31min**. Below and ahead of you is the little island, Peñas de Arabí, dwarfed by the towering cliffs of the Sierra Helada.

The path, clear but steep, and only about 10m/yds from the cliff edge, zigzags down into the next gully, before rising again past the ruins of what was probably an animal pen (**2h**). After crossing the small hump by the ruins, it descends to cross another gully. From here a steep climb (sometimes on all fours!) brings you to the penultimate peak (**2h30min**), from where you can see the asphalt road to the relay station. Now the path descends into the last gully, moves away from the cliffs, and joins the road (**2h40min**). Turn right and follow the road steeply uphill.

The relay station surrounds are closed, and you descend from the sierra about 50m/yds below its gates. Watch for your descent path, on the left (**3h**). It is fairly clear and, once on it, you will see red marking, sometimes supplemented by green arrows. The resort and beach at Albir lie far below, and the path heads in that general direction, initially contouring below the relay station. It passes under electricity cables and begins to descend steeply. Ignore short-cuts as it zigzags down, following the line of the cables. When the path forks (**3h10min**), go right through a pine wood. After an open, fairly level section, the path splits again (**3h20min**): take either fork — they meet up again about five minutes later.

Eventually you wind down to a five-way junction, at a flattish piece of ground level with apartments on the left (**3h35min**). Go right and keep following the cables, ignoring all crossing paths. You can see the road to the Albir lighthouse passing through a tunnel below and you reach this road, called Camí Vell del Far, directly under the cables, at **3h45min**. Follow the road to the left as it winds towards Albir's promenade. Cross the main road by the cafés and bars, and turn right to the bus stop which is about 100m/yds away (**4h**).

6 SERPIS GORGE

Distance: 20km/12.4mi; 5h   **See also photographs pages 26, 63**

Grade: easy, level, out-and-back walk along the route of an old railway line. Fairly long, with some tunnels to go through

Equipment: see page 42; also torch

How to get there and return: 🚌 to L'Orxa (the 72km-point on Car tour 2). Just before the bridge over the Serpis River, on the western outskirts of the village, turn left uphill and park at the old station.

Short walk: Castell de Perputxent. 1km/0.6mi; 40min. Easy. Equipment as page 42; access as main walk. Climb the steep rocky path about 30m/yds to the right of L'Orxa station (past a sign reading 'La Solana'), to the castle shown on pages 26 and 63 (20min). A gap between the walls and one of its two existing towers provides entry to the interior.

Alternative walk: Serpis Circuit. 15km/9.3mi; 4h10min. Strenuous ascent/descent of 350m/1150ft. Equipment, access as main walk. Follow the main walk to the 1h38min-point, then take the waymarked path to the right. Clamber over a few rocks, then wind steeply up through abandoned terraces and past a waterfall. Carefully follow the waymarkings up and alongside a house (2h05min) and then to a concrete track, where you turn right. The surface changes to dirt, then asphalt. Keep to the asphalt past several houses but, just after two houses on the left, turn sharp right at a junction (signposted to L'Orxa). Shortly afterwards (at a large ornate house), turn right on a track. Climb steeply to an open area on a crest (2h35min), where there is a chained gate on the right and a path up left to the summit of Safor. Take the track straight ahead. You have joined Walk 7 at its 1h35min point. Use the map to follow Walk 7 (in reverse) down to L'Orxa (4h). At the road, turn right to your car.

T his pleasant riverside stroll through the picturesque Serpis Gorge can be enjoyed by anyone. From the level track you can appreciate the marked contrast between the sheer cliffs surrounding the gorge and the gentleness of the river flowing through it. The river valley provides an ideal habitat for wild flowers and birds — so allow a full day for picnicking, botanising and birdwatching.

Start the walk from L'Orxa station by following the old railway line below the castle. Just after a

Second dam on the Serpis (1h38min)

bend, alongside a little ruined house (**9min**), ignore a track off to the right (**P**6a); continue through extensive olive terraces to the first of the tunnels (**30min**). This is quite long, but soon after entering you can see the other end.

You emerge in a gentle landscape with low trees and, in spring, wild flowers everywhere. The heavily-reeded river banks are alive with the song of Cetti's warblers in spring and summer, and crag martins swoop hither and thither as they catch their food on the wing. Fish, some of them unbelievably large, swim unconcernedly in the clear water, and grey herons feed well.

At **46min** a path goes off right to a dam (**P**6b) — the source of the *canaleta* that runs along to the rather grand old hydroelectric station on the opposite side of the river (as you approach it, you will see and hear water cascading down a channel from the *canaleta* above). Leave the track at **1h14min**: go down towards the river and cross it on a low bridge. Just past the chained entrance to the hydro-electric station (now a water quality control station), take a small path up to a pretty, ruined *ermita*.

Continue along the track, the river now on your left. You rejoin the railway line at an old ruined bridge (**1h 23min**), where it used to cross the river. Lush orange groves lie between you and the river, before you go through a very short tunnel (**1h28min**). After two houses, and just opposite the dam shown on page 59, note a walkers' signpost indicating a steep path up to the right (**1h38min**; *route of the Alternative walk*). Continue straight ahead here, through the next tunnel (**1h41min**) — not much more than a wide arch. Soon you will reach a bridge over an open grassy area (**1h49min**) with paths down to the river — a place favoured by local camping groups. It's an obvious spot to take a break.

Then continue along the track and through a cutting. There are more orange groves down by the river and another *canaleta* runs along the opposite bank. At **1h55min** negotiate another tunnel — it's quite long, but you can see the exit straight away.

The last of the tunnels is encountered at **2h05min**; it's the longest (500m/0.3mi), but can be avoided: just before the entrance, scramble a couple of metres/yards down the slope to the left, then walk along a narrow path to the far end. You will pass a ruined building, probably an old mill, on the river bank before rejoining the railway line (**2h14min**).

Now high above the river, follow the railway through pine woods, until you come to the end of the line — another dismantled bridge (**2h30min**). Standing on top of the old supports, you have a glorious panoramic view of the amphitheatre created by the high, rugged peaks and sheer cliffs of Safor.

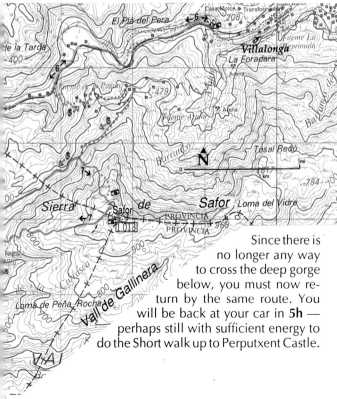

Since there is no longer any way to cross the deep gorge below, you must now return by the same route. You will be back at your car in **5h** — perhaps still with sufficient energy to do the Short walk up to Perputxent Castle.

7 SIERRA DE SAFOR

See map pages 60-61   **Distance:** 13km/8mi; 5h20min

Grade: fairly strenuous, with an ascent and corresponding descent of 765m/2500ft. Paths are good and navigation straightforward.

Equipment: see page 42; also compass

How to get there and return: 🚌 to L'Orxa (the 72km-point on Car tour 2). Shortly after crossing the Serpis River, on the western outskirts of the village, park on the right at the Font Grota — alongside a small garden with stone tables.

Short walk: L'Orxa — Font dels Olbits — L'Orxa. 7km/4.3mi; 2h20min. Easy climb and descent of 290m/950ft. Equipment as page 42; access as main walk. Follow the main walk for 1h, then take the path on the right to the Font dels Olbits. Return the same way.

Approaching from the west, Safor looks fairly gentle but, from the north, its jagged peaks and sheer cliffs present quite a different spectacle. Its ascent offers a variety of experiences and scenery. Just below the summit there is a *nevera* and, on the way down, you can take a relaxing break at the picturesque Font dels Olbits.

Start out at the Font Grota: cross the road and turn right on the track which runs along the far side of the wide old river bed, now concreted. Pass two small footbridges, then turn left up the track just beyond the last house in the row. Immediately, take the narrow footpath which zigzags up to the right. When you reach a track (**6min**) turn right. You will now follow this winding track uphill for more than an hour, so relax and enjoy the scenery as it unfolds around successive bends. In **15min**, looking back to the southwest, you enjoy the view shown below. After a while the track levels out (**24min**) and skirts above the Barranc del Bassiete. About 10 minutes later, down to the left, you have a brief view of the Serpis Gorge (Walk 6). After passing some large almond terraces at the head of the *barranco*, the Font dels Olbits becomes visible ahead, set into the lower slopes of Safor (**46min**). At this point ignore a signposted track to the right and continue to enjoy the magnificent series of vistas. Listen for the rattle of corn buntings in the shrubs and trees around you and look for Dartford warblers — they nest in this area.

After 15 minutes' climbing, you look back over L'Orxa against the backdrop of Montcabrer. Benicadell rises to the right.

As the track passes between patches of well-cultivated land, watch for a huge galvanised iron water tank on the left (**1h**). Just opposite the tank, a path goes to the right alongside an almond grove and leads to the Font dels Olbits. We visit it on the return from Safor, *but the Short walk turns right here.* Continue eastwards on the main track, with variable surfacing underfoot. Ignore a track to the right and, later, a concreted track going down into the valley to the left (**1h15min**).

You come to an open area on the left, with a chained gateway (**1h35min**; *Alternative walk 6 comes in here*). To begin the ascent of Safor, locate a waymarked path going up the ridge to your right. It is well-trodden, but very steep: take it slowly. As you ascend, take careful note when you reach some crags (**1h50min**) that your path splits into two. Both forks go to the same place. The path to the left, through rocks, is waymarked. However, we prefer the right-hand path. The paths rejoin (**2h20min**) and, shortly afterwards, you enjoy a magnificent view of the broad amphitheatre formed by the northern face of Safor. Nearby, the 'eye of the needle' — a natural rock arch — frames another view, down over the coastal plain.

Continue the ascent and reach a flat grassy 'meadow' just below the summit (**2h50min**). Here you can investigate the remains of an underground *nevera* (snow well), before the final, 10-minute ascent up the obvious path to the cross and trig point on Safor (1013m/3325ft; **3h**). From this summit much of the Costa Blanca is visible below. Ahead, the *huerta* spreads out its blanket of cultivation. To the northeast lies Gandía and the high-rise developments of the *playas*; the River Serpis (Walk 6) flows in the north. The western skyline is pierced by the distinctive peak of Benicadell. The reservoir at Beniarrés glimmers in the southwest, while the Vall de Gallinera spreads across the southern front, with the massed ranks of the sierras of Alicante beyond it. Finally, Montgó (Walk 1) rises to the southeast, with Denia and Jávea at its feet.

Retrace your steps to the meadow and take care here

While at L'Orxa visit the old station (where Walk 6 begins) and the Castell de Perpuxtent above it.

to locate the correct path for the descent. Go along the meadow to the left (southwest). The main path at the end of the meadow goes straight ahead, but leads only into difficult terrain with some very deep potholes. Your path goes to the right just before entering the trees — be sure to find the clear yellow and white waymarks. From this point, the route down is clear. Follow the waymarked path, fairly level at first, but gradually getting steeper as it descends. At **3h55min** note a walkers' signpost and a track to the right — a short cut back to your outward route. But take the path ahead to the Font dels Olbits (**4h05min**).

When you leave the Font, you have two options. You can take the track leading round from the benches and, when you are just opposite the large water tank you passed on your outward route, take the path bridging the short distance back to your outward track. Alternatively, as you head away from the *font*, locate some steps on the left, with PR waymarks. They lead to a narrow path which winds downhill and crosses the *barranco*, to the *finca* on the opposite side. From the *finca* a track leads to the track you followed on the outward route. Whichever option you take, on reaching your outgoing track, turn left back down to L'Orxa (**5h20min**).

View from the Font dels Olbits. The area around the font (which has a year-round water supply), has been beautifully restored, with benches and tables from where you can enjoy this magnificent landscape. Terraces, now largely unexploited, cover the low hills, while Benicadell, sometimes likened to the Matterhorn, rises in the distance.

8 PONT DE LES CALDERES • BARRANCO DE LA ENCANTADA • ERMITA DE SANTO CRISTO • PONT DE LES CALDERES

Distance: 10km/6.2mi; 2h55min

Grade: easy, but the climb up to the *ermita* (140m/460ft) is quite strenuous. Paths and tracks are good; navigation is straightforward.

Equipment: see page 42

How to get there and return: 🚌 to/from the Pont de les Calderes, at the 18km marker on the C3311 between Muro and Pego (the 53km-point on Car tour 2). Park well off the road, just to the west of the bridge, opposite a defaced sign indicating the road down to the Barranco de la Encantada and a newer sign, 'Camí de l'Almadec'.

Short walk: Barranco de la Encantada. 4km/2.5mi; 1h16min. Easy. Equipment and access as above. Follow the main walk to the mill (38min) and return the same way.

In addition to exceptional views, this delightful walk offers a peaceful stroll by a stream, deep pools under the imposing cliffs of an impressive gorge, an optional detour to Planes with its ancient aqueduct and Moorish castle, and an old pilgrimage trail to an *ermita*. Autumn, when the heather is purple on the hillsides and trees in the valleys shine yellow and gold, is the best time of year.

Begin the walk by following the signposted road to the Barranco de la Encantada; it is asphalted at first, but not in good condition. Descending slightly through orchards, it leads (**10min**) to a ruined *casita* and your first glimpse of water in the *barranco* on the right. A little further on, you pass a ford across the watercourse, and the cliffs of the gorge begin to appear. The sound of running water accompanies you, as the gorge becomes deeper. In **15min** wooden steps beckon you down to the first of the pools, but only a minute ahead are the steps to the main pools (**P**8a). Calcium salts give the water a green and cloudy look, but it is fresh and cool.

Continue along what is now a track and, as you leave this narrow section of gorge, terracing opens out around you. The Sierra de la Albureca appears ahead, while to the right are the rugged crags of the Sierra de Foradá. At **24min** the track forks to the left of a newish white house and about a minute later peters out into a path, as it passes the black gates of Villa Mónica. Descending through a small orchard, the path leads you into the next stage of the Barranco de la Encantada — surprisingly reminiscent of a British landscape: a stream running through small green fields. You come upon pools, a tiny reservoir (**P**8b) and, at **31min**, another ruined *casita*. More rugged peaks are visible ahead as the gorge closes in.

From the Morro de la Encantada above the Barranco de la Encantada, there is a magnificent view of the church at Beniarrés, standing proud above the village. The Sierra de Benicadell fills in the background.

This is a popular walk so several paths have been created. As long as you keep the *barranco* on your right, you can take whichever you wish — they all lead to the same place — 'an old mill by the stream' (**38min**). The *barranco* becomes very deep and sheer at this point. *The Short walk turns back here.* The path climbs up to the left then levels out near the top of the cliff, with views down the remainder of the *barranco* to the Serpis River (**51min**).

Continue upwards through olive terraces to a small building. Walk past the gate at the right of the building (the fruit on the trees just below the gate, bright orange when ripe, is *kaki* — persimmon). Continue through the remainder of the terraces and turn left on the wide track you meet at the ridge (**1h01min**). But first spend a few minutes taking in the fantastic views below — the upper Serpis Valley, the Embalse de Beniarrés, and the magnificent Sierra de Benicadell almost straight ahead. Walk down the track in the setting shown above; Villa Isabelita (**1h09min**) commands the sort of views that most of us can only dream about.

At **1h33min** the village of Planes comes into view, built around its Moorish castle. As you meet the asphalt road, turn left; after about 200m/yds (just past the 1km marker), take steps up left (**1h38min**) to the Ermita de Santo Cristo.*

*Or first make a (high recommended) detour into Planes: continue down the road for 200m/yds, then take the road to the right. Cross the *barranco* and keep uphill to the *font* (still in use) and the aqueduct (10min). From here you can easily see your way through the village to the castle (10min). After the detour return to these steps to continue.

The first few steps are concrete, but the rest are hewn out of natural rock and make for an easy, though strenuous, ascent. Take it slowly, admire the views and count the stations of the cross as you go. The twelfth station appears at **2h**, as you meet the road which winds round the back of the hill from Planes. There is a thirteenth station just before the entrance to the *ermita,* where you will also find picnic benches and fantastic views.

Leave the *ermita* by heading downhill on the asphalt road. The Embalse de Beniarrés sparkles below and, if you are lucky, you may see Bonelli's eagles soaring above. They are resident in this area of Spain, and their white bodies and darker wings make them identifiable with the naked eye. At the crossroads (**2h11min**) go straight ahead on a narrow track, walking through mixed fruit orchards down into and across a *barranco.* Ignore all tracks going off into the terraces on the next section but, soon after the *barranco,* take the left-hand fork (the right fork goes up to a visible gatepost). Zigzag quite sharply uphill.

At **2h26min** a modern white house comes into view, and you meet another fork. This time take the track which climbs to the right. When it levels out, you can almost see down the Barranco de la Encantada again (behind a house on the left). A minute later, as you meet another track (**2h36min**), turn right. This track will take you down through heather-clad slopes all the way to your car. It follows a ridge, with the Barranco de la Encantada on the left and views over to the *ermita* and Planes on your right, providing a wonderful overview of the countryside traversed throughout the walk. You will see your car in the valley below and reach it at **2h55min**.

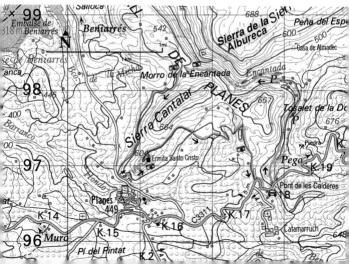

9 L'ATZUBIA • CASTELL DE GALLINERA • ALMISERA • L'ATZUBIA

Distance: 11km/6.8mi; 3h20min

Grade: fairly strenuous, with prolonged, sometimes steep, ascents and corresponding descents of 540m/1770ft. Tracks and paths are good; navigation is straightforward.

Equipment: see page 42

How to get there and return: 🚌 to L'Atzubia (Adsubia) on the C3311 5km west of Pego (the 97km-point on Car tour 2); park in the tiny square.

Short walks: Gallinera Castle. Fairly strenuous ascent/descent of 300m/ 980ft. Equipment, access as main walk. Follow the main walk to the first saddle and back (fine view of the castle; 5.5km/3.4mi; 1h45min) or go to the saddle below the castle and back (7km/4.3mi; 2h15min).

Alternative walk: L'Atzubia — Castell de Gallinera — Almiserá — L'Atzubia. 10km/6.2mi; 2h45min. Equipment, access and grade as main walk, but you must also be surefooted and have a head for heights. This walk covers the same ground as the main walk, but instead of skirting below the Almiserá cliffs on the track, it follows a narrow footpath (**danger of vertigo**). Follow the main walk to the track by Gallinera Castle (1h06min), where the main walk turns left. Here take a PR-waymarked path between the track and your outward path. This narrow and rocky path, clearly marked, leads under the northern cliffs of Almiserá. It crosses a few short scree runs horizontally, and leads to some beehives after about 30min. At the beehives, turn right on a track. On reaching an asphalt road, turn left and pick up the main walk at the 2h14min-point (notes on page 72).

This walk takes you through rural countryside, ascends an old mule trail, contours under imposing cliffs, and offers unbelievable views of one of the region's strategically-sited castles. Birdwatchers and botanists will find much to interest them in this varied terrain.

The walk starts in L'Atzubia's tiny main square, by the *font* just outside the Bar Cazadores (Hunters' Bar). Climb the road by the *font* (Calle Principal) all the way past the church. When you reach the steps by the cross, take the middle road, which bears slightly left. Despite being surfaced, this road sees little traffic. It takes you through the orange groves at the beginnings of the very fertile Gallinera Valley and alongside the Barranco de Michel down to your left. All the time you will be climbing steadily, so take it slowly and enjoy the pleasant country atmosphere. Ahead you can see the Castell de Gallinera and higher up, to its left, the TV antennas on top of Almiserá. Even further to the left, your return route is visible, snaking down the hillside. Ignore a road off to the left (**10min**) and start climbing a little more steeply.

At **18min**, as you go under the electricity lines, make sure to follow the road round a hairpin to the left, ignoring the track going straight ahead. Many of the terraces

On the approach to Gallinera Castle, 1h into the walk. You can take a 20min return detour to the castle, but it is privately owned and kept locked.

around here are cultivated with *algarrobas* — carob or locust beans; they are used for animal feed. Nowadays, however, this crop is less popular and rarely seen. The road zigzags up towards an obvious saddle below Almiserá, and you will have passed a few houses by the time it becomes a track (**29min**). It then winds steadily up the lower slopes of Almiserá, its antennas still visible above. The orange groves have been left far below; only carobs, olives and almonds grace these higher slopes.

You will probably already have noticed the little white *casita* clinging to the slopes above you to the left — you will pass this shortly. Looking back as you contour along one of the flatter sections, there is a good view of L'Atzubia, framed in the hills, with the coastal plain and the sea behind it. At a junction (**35min**) go uphill to the right. Just before reaching the power lines again, turn right on the track marked with a red arrow (**43min**). Ignore a track coming in from the left, and pass in front of the white *casita* (**46min**). Continue straight ahead on what is now just an old narrow mule trail which zigzags up over the terraces. Follow the red markers, ignoring a path coming in from the left just before reaching the saddle (**53min**), from where there is a superb view of Gallinera Castle. *The first Short walk option turns back here.*

From the saddle you can pick out the next part of your route going round the slopes towards the castle. The well-marked path is level at first, then it climbs through some old almond terraces. You pass to the left of a ruined *casita,* before levelling out a bit under a crag and joining a track on another saddle just below the castle (**1h06min**); see photograph and caption above. (This track goes all the way down into the valley, to the village of Benirrama, which claims the castle as its own and calls it Castell de Benirrama.) *The second Short walk turns back here.*

Turn left on the track, to circle under the imposing cliffs of Almiserá. *(The path here, lying between your upward route and the track you are now following, is the route of the Alternative walk.)* Yellow and white PR waymarks

69

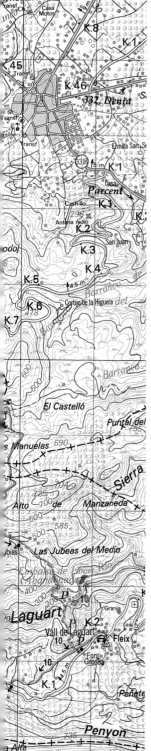

replace the red markings and as you set off on this new track, you have a magnificent view of the entire Gallinera Valley below you to the right. The track is initially wide, but in very poor condition after years of storm damage. In some parts rocky, in others just stony, it has been deeply furrowed by running water, and the presence of several large boulders indicates the instability of the cliffs above. As you proceed, the track deteriorates further — at times it is little more than a footpath. Your views of the castle, however, continue to improve!

Ignore paths off to the terraces and continue uphill beneath the cliffs, which are home to peregrine falcons and ravens. As you approach the plateau below Almiserá, the landscape opens out heralding a change in bird life — look out for black redstart, goldfinch and wheatear. At **1h45min** you are on the wide plateau which stretches between Vall de Gallinera and Vall d'Ebo and, if it is a Sunday or a *fiesta* in autumn, you may spot a number of *seta* (wild mushroom) gatherers foraging in the vegetation, baskets or buckets hanging hopefully over their arms.

At **1h53min** join a narrow surfaced road and turn left. At the top of the hill (**2h**) the energetic may like to turn left and climb up the road to the summit of Almiserá (757m/ 2480ft). But the main walk heads downhill to the right here, with Pego visible just beyond the valley below, and the coast clear in the distance. The crags of Almiserá loom starkly on the left as the road winds quite steeply down towards Pego. At **2h09min**, on a particularly sharp hairpin bend to the left, there is a small open area with a large boulder. A narrow path goes straight ahead and provides a fragrant short cut which avoids that long bend. Rejoin the road five minutes later (**2h14min**); *the Alternative walk comes in here.* The rocky hillsides are carpeted with herbs, dwarf palms, gorse and heather, and you will pass several *casitas*, including one on the left with an attractive well.

At **2h23min** turn left on a narrow road (where there is a fire risk warning sign). This is your road back into L'Atzubia. Follow it past some houses before reaching the top of a small rise, from where you have a view of L'Atzubia nestling in the valley below. It's a long way down, so the road zigzags steeply — very hard on the knees! It is in such a poor state of repair that we have never met any vehicles on it. As you drop through the terraces there are wide views down the sheer slopes into the valley. At **3h** giant reeds line a small *barranco,* and the *algarrobas* and almonds give way to orange and cherry trees. At **3h13min** the road crosses another *barranco* and takes you straight up a short steep rise, back to the *font* in L'Atzubia; you are back at your car in **3h20min**.

10 SIERRA DE LA CARRASCA AND THE MOZARABIC TRAILS

See map pages 70-71; see also photograph page 12

Distance: 23km/14.3mi; 6h50min

Grade: long and strenuous, with ascents and corresponding descents of 900m/2950ft. A couple of stretches require careful navigation. *Only recommended in the cooler seasons.*

Equipment: see page 42; also compass, towel, picnic, plenty of water

How to get there and return: ⛟ to Fleix (the 122km-point on Car tour 1); park at the school, at the far (western) end of the village.

Short walk: Mozarabic trail. 2.5km/1.5mi; 1h10min. Easy descent/strenuous re-ascent of 180m/590ft. Equipment, access as *Alternative walk.* Follow the *Alternative walk* to the falls (30min); return the same way.

Alternative walk: Embalse de Isbert. 5.5km/3.4mi; 2h40min. Strenuous descent/reascent of 260m/850ft. In summer, the bed of the Río Ebo can be a furnace; do *not* attempt this outside the cool season. Access and equipment as main walk, but no compass required. Follow the main walk to the *lavadero* (5min; **P**10b), then take the path down to the right 30m/yds further on — the beginning of the Mozarabic trail shown below. Descend through a cave to the base of a waterfall (30min; **P**10c) and continue down to the river bed (45min; **P**10d). Turn right and wind downstream through this amazing gorge to the Embalse de Isbert (1h 15min). Most of the year this reservoir is completely dry — hence its popular name, 'Isbert's Folly'. Return the same way.

If you are fit enough to tackle a really long, full-day walk, then do not miss this one. It has everything! It takes you along the Vall de Laguart, over the barren Carrasca Ridge and into Vall d'Ebo for a break in one of the bars. After crossing the Barranco del Infierno, you return on a pair

The Mozarabic trail, seen from the rock arch (6h15min into the main walk, but only 25min from Fleix; Alternative walk and Picnics 10c-d). The word Mozarabic ('would-be Arab') refers to Christians who were allowed to practise their religion under Moorish rule. To get around in the mountainous terrain they built narrow trails which were cleverly stepped so that the usual difficulties associated with steep ascents and descents were minimised. Natural rock was used where possible, but for the most part they represent a remarkable feat of design and construction. Some have since fallen into decline and others have been lost to vegetation, sometimes coming to light by chance or after a severe fire. But many remain in good order today and are a feature of several of the walks in this book.

of Mozarabic trails, one plunging steeply down into the bed of the Ebo, the other thrusting back up again. *For less hardy souls, the Alternative walk is no less exhilarating.*

Begin by continuing along the road past the school (yellow and white waymarks). Almost immediately, take a track to the right. Pass Font Grossa and the *lavadero*, the village wash-house shown on page 12 (**5min**; *P*10b). Some 30m/yds further on, the path down to the right is your return route *(turn down right here for the Alternative walk or P10c, d)*. Continue winding gently up through almond groves, past another *font* and *lavadero* just below Benimaurell. Climb steeply into this village (**29min**) and head around to the right (past the Bar Oasis) as you leave it on a narrow country road. As you gain height and skirt a metal fence, notice the Sierra del Penyon (or Caballo Verde) on the left, the Barranco del Infierno on the right and the barren Carrasca Ridge ahead. Pass a *font* with picnic tables (**43min**) and continue to a col — the highest point on this stretch of road (**1h09min**). Just over the top are two tiny *casitas*, each with a well (**1h13min**).

Then turn right on a track which edges the right-hand side of a restored *finca*. You are heading (eventually) for Carrasca, the ridge which looms on your right. Ignore a track to the left (**1h18min**) and continue to an animal pen below on a saddle (**1h24min**). You are now at the head of two valleys; on the right, running northeast, is the Vall de Laguart; on the left, running southwest, is the beginning of the Jalón Valley. You are making for another small saddle ahead, at the top of the Carrasca Ridge.

Some 50m/yds past the pen, leave the track: take a path on the left. It is indistinct at first (sheep have created several paths in the area), but you can see it snaking up the right-hand side of the little hillock ahead. After flanking this hillock, head for a rocky outcrop some 300m/yds away (slightly to the right). When you get there, identify your next objective: a cluster of rocks ahead to the right. An obvious path leads diagonally uphill to them; it stands out clearly from the darker vegetation surrounding it. Walk straight ahead, maintaining height, to reach this path, and then pass to the left of the rocks (**1h43min**) — perhaps disturbing a noisy chough down in the valley.

From this point, there are some yellow waymarks. If you are walking just after summer rains, you will be greeted by a carpet of meadow saffron crocuses. The path becomes indistinct for about 50m/yds as it goes slightly to the left and across a *barranco*. It then heads diagonally northeast, along the front of the ridge, and gently gains height. *Take care to keep with the yellow markings — if you lose them, go back to the previous one and locate the continuation.* A right-angle mark signals a change of direction: the first of these is at **1h55min**. The path passes beneath some prominent rocks, about 2m/6ft high, just below the crest of the ridge (**2h01min**). Immediately after these high rocks, don't miss a sharp left turn. From here the waymarks are rather difficult to see, but you can forget them and climb the remaining 20m/65ft or so to the saddle at the top of the ridge (**2h05min**). Vall d'Ebo is far below and you can see along the coast from Denia to Gandía. Across the valley, on the Gallinera Ridge, locate the summit of Almiserá, with its TV antenna.

On the same line of sight, but only about 20m/yds ahead of you, yellow paint indicates the continuation of your path. It is again a little difficult to see in places as the vegetation is more plentiful on this moister side of the ridge, but it contours to the right about 20m/yds below the top of the ridge — heading northeast. It takes you up and round the left of a rocky hillock about 500m/0.3mi away. Don't worry unduly if you lose the paint marks on this stretch — just make your way to the left slope of the hillock (**2h13min**), beyond which you see Almiserá and the TV antenna. Here you leave the path and the way-marking: freewheel down the wide flat ridge, heading west of north and keeping Almiserá ahead to the right. The village of Vall d'Ebo can be seen (**2h18min**) below and slightly to the right of the direction in which you are walking. This ridge, a spur off the main Carrasca sierra, will take you all the way down off the mountain.

The terrain makes for easy walking, but take care when the descent becomes a little steeper, with *barrancos* on either side. To the left of Vall d'Ebo village you'll see a *finca* with a red-tiled roof; in front of it there is a little stone shelter surrounded by extensive almond and olive terraces. Make your way down to the top terrace (**2h 39min**), then circle left and downhill through the terraces to the shelter. From here, locate another small building on the opposite side of a *barranco* and contour round to it (**2h55min**). Pass just to the right of this building and continue round the groves, skirting to the left of a small hillock, until you reach a farm track just below. Turn right towards a *finca* and reach an asphalt road (**3h04min**). Follow it downhill to the right, into Vall d'Ebo (**3h20min**).

Refreshment is available in the village, but if you have

a picnic, press on*. Past the sports centre and camp ground, turn left to a bridge over the Ebo (**3h23min**). Don't cross it; turn right along the river. At the next bridge, turn right, then sharp left (yellow and white waymarks). Continue along the river, past the cemetery on your right (**3h33min**). A track takes you past a ford, to a junction (**3h39min**). If water is flowing, there is a good picnic spot by the river five minutes along the left fork (**P**10a). We head *right* here (signposted 'Vall de Laguart'), to Font Xili (**3h44min**), another setting for **P**10a, where we can refill our water bottles.

From Font Xili the track continues high above the bed of the Barranco del Infierno. Watch out on the left (**3h 50min**) for your clear, waymarked path descending to the river bed, going straight across, and winding along the opposite bank. The views of the river bed become ever more spectacular as you descend. The path drops quite sharply before passing a ruined house on the right, and then climbs steeply through almond groves to a newer house (**4h20min**). Join the track leading from this house and meet a major track after a further 200m/yds.

Turn right; the track (still waymarked) takes you around the head of a *barranco*, past a crumbling house on the right, with a well (**4h38min**). Soon (**4h44min**) you will spot several ruined buildings on the far side of a little ravine — the Corrales de Carrasca. Later, rounding the top of some almond terraces, you have a good view into the Barranco del Infierno, as you approach a pine-clad hillside. Where the track starts to descend below the pine wood, it can be quite wet underfoot. Once down in the 'dip' (**5h10min**), turn right on a waymarked path to the Pozo de las Jubias, a well with five stone animal troughs.

Pass the well and descend a path on the left (close to the wall). This is the beginning of your long zigzag descent into the bed of the Ebo on the Mozarabic trail shown on pages 72-73. After a while, look for the twin trail winding up the far side to your final destination, Fleix, and, part-way up, a waterfall — which must be imagined unless there has been heavy rain! Cross the (usually dry) river bed (**5h55min**; **P**10d) and then zigzag up the far side, passing beneath the waterfall (**6h10min**) and under very steep cliffs (**P**10c). Go through a huge arch cut in the rock by the Mozarabs, pass across the top of the waterfall, and stagger up to the top (**6h44min**). Turn left to the *lavadero* and main road, then left again to your car (**6h50min**).

*If you have been in the village centre, head east from Plaza Mayor until you reach the second (waymarked) bridge mentioned in the text.

11 VUELTA DEL SOMO (SOMO CIRCUIT)

Distance: 11km/6.8mi; 3h24min

Grade: moderate, with ascents and corresponding descents of 260m/850ft. Good surfaces underfoot and straightforward navigation.

Equipment: see page 42

How to get there and return: 🚌 from Benidorm: take the C3318 north and turn left just past Tárbena, on the AV1203. Park in front of a building on the right about 100m before the 3km marker (the 93km-point on Car tour 3).

For variety of terrain, overwhelming views and outstanding scenery, this walk comes near the top of the list. While Somo itself is an unremarkable mountain, as you make this anticlockwise circuit it becomes obvious why this is one of our favourite walks. Look out for golden eagles which hunt in the area ... and for the tracks of the wild boar so prized by hunters.

Start out by crossing the road from the building: take a track towards some houses (the Casas de Bijauca). Ignore tracks which lead to the houses and concentrate on the view ahead. You are making for the saddle to the west, where there is an orange building, and will then go around the back of Somo, the hill to its left, and return through the valley. As the track sweeps left at a ruined house on the right (**5min**), take the concrete track straight

Bollula Castle rises on a ridge beyond almond groves, just 20min into the walk. To catch the almond trees in blossom, walk in early February. In April, cherry blossom will feature throughout this walk.

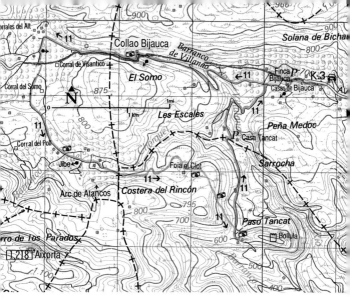

ahead. Just at the far side of more ruins (Finca Bijauca; **8min**), there is an open grassy area (**P**11a). But take a path a few metres/yards *before* the picnic spot, going downhill between drystone walls, to a track and a well (**11min**). Turn right and 200m/yds further on, fork right on another track (**14min**; you will return from the track on the left at the end of the walk). Concreted in places, the track heads west through the almond groves shown on page 77, parallel with the road on which you parked.

Ignore a track to the left just before the Barranco de Villanao and another to the right, as you walk above the *barranco*, which you cross at **26min**. The track, now almost a path, sweeps left and appears to be going in the wrong direction. But it is just gaining height and will soon zigzag round to the west again. At **40min** join a track which enters from the left and climbs gently past a galvanised water tank to the road (**46min**).

Turn left and climb to the saddle you saw earlier — the Collao Bijauca (**54min**), from where the peaks of Serrella rise ahead in the west. Descend towards the foot of the hill, to a 'Coto Privado de Caza' sign on the right (**1h**). Turn right on the track here; it takes you on a gentle stroll through flat rural countryside. At a junction where there is a collection of houses (Corrales del Alt; **1h09min**), turn left and head directly towards the craggy ridge of Aixorta. Fork left (**1h11min**) past a well and reach the road again (**1h15min**). Watch out around here for corn buntings; their rattling call is unmistakable. Cross the road and take the wide track a few metres/yards to the left (just opposite the

7km marker); head towards Aixorta. This is a popular spot for people gathering *setas* (wild mushrooms) in autumn.

The track, waymarked with yellow and white, climbs gradually past a small pine wood and through almond groves to a *casita* and house on the right (**1h31min**). The Arc de Atancos, a rock arch, is visible ahead. Soon the track splits: go left and, about 20m/yds further on, ignore a minor track going left to some ruins. Your marked track goes downhill into the beginning of the Barranco del

Chorquet. Off to the right, in a stony stream bed, there is a well, the Jibe de Chorquet (**1h35min**). (Just past the well, enthusiasts could take a 40min return detour: follow a track on the right. It leads to a point below the Arc de Atancos from where it is possible to clamber up the way-marked rocks to take a closer look at the arch.)

The main walk goes straight ahead here, following the Barranco del Chorquet. As the track sweeps downhill to the left, take a narrow waymarked path on the right, edging an almond grove (**1h40min**). You will follow this narrow path for some time as it skirts around the Costera del Rincón, the Barranco del Chorquet deep on the left.

At **1h49min** a huge cave comes into view on the far side of the *barranco,* and the path rounds some extensive but abandoned terraces. Pass a ruined *casita* as you cross a shallow valley, the Foia El Clot (**2h**). Then climb a rather desolate hillside to a crest (**2h06min**), from where you enjoy a first good view of the sheer cliffs of Paso Tancat ('Closed Gorge'). Descending, the views encompass the high peaks of the Bernia Ridge to the southeast, Bolulla Castle on its craggy ridge and the Sierra Helada to the south, close to Benidorm. Across the valley, to the left, you can see your homeward track snaking up to the houses around Finca Bijauca and, on the valley floor, a *finca* which you will reach later in the walk.

The path continues round the Costera del Rincón, all the while losing a little height, until it reaches a saddle (**2h30min**), where it meets a track coming up from the valley. You will turn down left here, but first go over the saddle and look at the old settlement which locals call 'the high place'. Several ruined houses are still in reasonable condition, and merit exploring. From the saddle the crags below Bolulla Castle rise impressively above you.

Return to the track and descend it. Paso Tancat almost defies belief from this vantage point, so sheer are its cliffs. Ignore a track off right to terraces just before a short uphill section, and continue down to the valley floor. Soon after passing some olive groves a path goes right (**2h53min**) to Casa Tancat, the *finca* you saw from above. Surrounded by cherry groves, it is a perfect spot for a break (***P***11b).

From here the track climbs steeply out of the valley. Looking back, you can marvel at the terrain you have just crossed. Just beyond some grassy terraces and a shed set amongst pines (**3h13min**), you reach the well passed on the outward route. Turn left up the path and then right on the concrete track, back to your car (**3h24min**).

12 FONTS DE L'ALGAR • SIERRA DE BERNIA • BARRANCO DE VINARREAL • FONTS DE L'ALGAR

See map pages 78-79   **Distance:** 17km/10.5mi; 5h10min

Grade: moderate-strenuous, with ascents and corresponding descents of 440m/1440ft. Good terrain underfoot. Navigation is straightforward, except on leaving the Vinarreal Valley, where care is needed.

Equipment: see page 42; also long trousers

How to get there and return: 🚌 to/from Casa Federico, Restaurante Bar La Cascada in Fonts de l'Algar (the 159km-point on Car tour 1).

Short walk: Waterfall above Fonts de l'Algar. 4km/2.5mi; 1h25min. Moderate climb/descent of 180m/590ft. Equipment as page 42; access as main walk. Follow the main walk for 43min (*P*12b), then return.

Alternative walk: Fonts de l'Algar — Sierra de Bernia — Fonts de l'Algar. 8.5km/5.2mi; 3h. Moderate-strenuous, with ascents and corresponding descents of 300m/980ft. Equipment as page 42; access as main walk. Follow the main walk to the1h49min-point, then cross the valley and wind uphill to a track where there is a well to the left and a ruined house to the right. Turn left just past the house; you have rejoined the main walk at the 4h18min-point.

This walk takes you through two fertile valleys, where the varied countryside is quite gentle despite being surrounded by rugged and barren sierras. Other highlights include a waterfall, the impressive Paso de los Bandoleros (Brigands' Pass) and a Mozarabic trail. Birdwatchers and botanists will find find much of interest, particularly in spring, and even if you don't actually see wild boar you will notice evidence of their presence.

Start out in the car park of Casa Federico. Go along by the water, past two small waterfalls (*P*12a) and into a narrow asphalt road with yellow and white PR waymarks. This road bears right (**3min**) and starts to climb very steeply. Ignore tracks to groves of oranges and *nísperos* (medlars) or houses; continue up until you pass a PR sign indicating that you are on the Travesia Severino (**19min**). From here the road is almost level. As you stop for a breather, look back to Campana, Ponoch, Aitana and Aixorta. Penya Severino (the end of the Sierra Bernia) and Ferrer rise to the right, their cliffs separated by a narrow vertical gap — the Paso de los Bandoleros.

At a fork (**23min**) go right, heading directly towards Penya Severino and the Bernia Ridge. Walk through orange groves and, just after passing a water reservoir (**29min**), turn right on a track which drops down into the valley. A steep concrete stretch takes you to the valley floor and through an avocado orchard, to a junction (**36min**). The main walk eventually goes left here but, first, a waterfall to the right is worth a visit. After crossing the

Waterfall at Algar (Picnic 12b). You don't see many in the Costa Blanca, so sit on the rocks for a while and enjoy this one — playground for robins and other small birds.

dry bed of the Algar River you will hear the sound of water ahead and see the gates leading to the control area. Before the gates (just after passing a disused dam), go down into the rocky river bed and make your way to the falls shown above (**43min**; *P*1 2b).

Retrace your steps to the junction and fork right. *(The Short walk heads left here, to return.)* When the track forks three ways, take the middle track and continue through more avocado groves. Ignore tracks into the groves and when your track splits again (**54min**) go straight ahead, leaving the orchards behind. A minute later, where a track goes straight ahead down into the valley, turn sharp right on another track, climbing steeply. There are good views of Campana and Ponoch through the cleft formed by the Algar. The track zigzags up, then levels out and runs parallel with the Algar Valley. At a junction where there is a large ruined *finca* on the left (**1h28min**), go straight ahead and slightly downhill on a track— towards another house, beautifully sited on a little spur (**1h33min**).

The track now winds down past abandoned houses (diggings of wild boar are particularly evident here) to the valley floor (**1h49min**). Just before crossing the river bed, take the narrow track off to the right. *(But for the Alternative walk, go left and cross the valley.)* This rocky track, at times just a path, runs into the river bed and bears right. Walk along the river bed for about 200m/yds, looking out for some houses above you on the left. When you reach them, take a path to the left, cross the river bed after about 100m/yds, and follow the right bank. After a further 200m/yds cross back to the left bank — at the confluence of the Algar and Vinarreal valleys (**1h58min**).*

Continue on the (sometimes overgrown) track which

---

*It is possible to follow the brigands' route along the Algar River by taking the path to the right which criss-crosses the river bed all the way to the Paso de los Bandoleros. It is rough, indistinct and overgrown. But on reaching the Paso you will be confronted by a high cliff and be unable to go any further without ropes.

bears left up the narrow Barranco de Vinarreal, a little-frequented valley. We have seen wild boar here … and a golden eagle soaring above Ferrer. Put on your long trousers: prickly gorse invades the track — now little more than a path. After heavy rain, you might get your feet wet, too, if there is water in the *barranco* bed. At **2h08min** pass the first *finca* up on the left, with well-kept terraces and carob trees. A long-abandoned Range Rover (however did it get here?) marks **2h16min**.

The track becomes overgrown once more and passes through pines, before reaching an open area from where the awesome peaks of Ferrer rise on your right (**2h28min**). As the valley begins to open out, the Carrascal de Parcent fills in the background. Continue alongside the *barranco*, to an open area where goats graze. Just past here, the waters of the *barranco* have forged two separate courses, now separated by giant reeds. When they join again, go straight ahead and meet a good track coming in from the right (**2h39min**). Turn left and follow the running stream on your left. Pass vegetable gardens on your right and notice the black pipes running alongside the stream. The point where they cross it is also your crossing point (**2h43min**). One of the pipes goes all the way up out of the valley; you will join it further up, but the first part of its route is overgrown and cannot be followed.

After crossing the stream climb up on to the first of several terraces. A small path takes you (always heading right then upwards), to a second, third and fourth terrace. Cross this fourth terrace to the left, and watch for faded red waymarking on the rock beside the path: follow it up to the fifth terrace. Head right along the fifth terrace, through thick gorse, and immediately look directly ahead (almost due west) to two rocky outcrops with two white houses below them. The house below the left-hand outcrop has an orange-tiled roof, and you will eventually pass about 100m/yds to the left of it. As you proceed, a third rocky outcrop appears to the left of the other two, and the path becomes overgrown and often indistinct. It goes up and right across two more terraces and then along the right-hand side of a wall. At a rough fork it bears right along the edge of a terrace, before climbing to the left and on to the next terrace where it makes its way through gorse and pines. When it becomes rocky and starts to climb, you will know you have reached a Mozarabic trail (**2h59min**; see notes in caption on page 73).

This trail is a little overgrown in places, but from now

on your way is clear. At a fork — the end of the overgrown section — go right, up alongside terraces. As you pass to the left of the house with the orange-tiled roof, the black pipe appears again, along the edge of the trail. Cross the track to the house and continue ahead, to another track (**3h03min**). Turn left here, leaving the Mozarabic trail (which continues steeply all the way up to the outskirts of Tárbena). Almost immediately ignore a track going up to the right; contour around the hillside, enjoying views to the left over the Vinarreal Valley. Just after passing a ruined house (**3h12min**), fork right on a track. But this track only goes up to the well behind the house, and you should go straight ahead on a level terrace — an old track which has been ploughed up and will be muddy in wet weather. Eventually a path is visible as you make your way along the terrace. When the path ends, look for another well — on the right and one terrace higher up (**3h17min**). Climb up and pass in front of the well. Continue to the end of this terrace, from where you can see — about 100m/yds away, at the far side of more terracing — a *casita* and your ongoing track.

A narrow hunters' path takes you up to the right and along one of the upper terraces, to the *casita* (**3h24min**). Now follow the track around the next valley, with Bernia directly ahead. When the track forks (**3h29min**), go left downhill. As you round the next bend ignore the track coming in from the left; vine terraces are ahead of you. Turn right when you join a track coming up from the valley (**3h34min**) and zigzag above the vines. Ignore a track going off to the left at a house (**3h42min**). Climb to a four-way junction (**3h51min**), from where your view stretches all the way along the Algar Valley towards Campana and Ponoch. Go straight ahead on the middle track. Pass a house on the left and continue winding downhill, high above the Algar Valley, past some ruins and towards the Paso de los Bandoleros. Walk under electricity cables (**4h10min**) and through pines, before reaching a ruined house on the right (**4h18min**). Just *before* the house, go right on a track. *(The Alternative walk rejoins here, from the left.)* After passing through groves of avocados and oranges and alongside a *finca* on the right, meet a narrow asphalt road (**4h29min**). Follow it past the turn-off to the waterfall, just before the small reservoir (**4h44min**). Now back on your outward route, continue down Travesia Severino, following the PR signs, into Fonts de l'Algar (**5h10min**).

13 VALLEYS OF THE SIERRA DE AITANA

Distance: 10km/6.2mi; 2h25min

Grade: easy, apart from a steady climb of 300m/980ft during the first 45 minutes; all on good clear tracks

Equipment: see page 42

How to get there and return: 🚌 or 🚐 to Guadalest. To the west of the village, pass the road to Benidorm and turn left up a narrow road signposted to El Trestellador restaurant (the 33km-point on Car tour 3). Pass the restaurant after about 1km and half a kilometre further on reach Font Molí, a small cluster of houses, with the old mill on the right. Turn right at the open area with room to park beside the wooden fence. The *font* and picnic tables are just above you (*P*13a).

Short walk: See page 86.

Much of this walk is a pleasant stroll through a series of high-altitude valleys, offering a variety of interesting features. Birdwatchers in particular can look forward to some worthwhile sightings. Don't be put off by the climbing on the first stage. Just take your time and enjoy the surroundings.

Start out by walking up the road which passes to the

About halfway through the walk, you leave the main route and continue through almond groves to Partagás, a tiny valley below a spur of Aitana. Here there are a few houses, picnic benches and a font (Fuente de Partagás), where you can refill your water bottles.

left of two picnic benches. Ahead are more benches and, on the left, the *font* (*P*13a). It gives a steady trickle of water, but the main flow is directed down a *canaleta* into the village. Just before the *font,* take a rough path up the hill to the left. Meet a track (**3min**) and turn right, to start your steady climb to the base of Penya Mulero. At **6min** the track forks. The main track goes straight ahead (*P*13b), but you must turn sharp right and pass through a chained gateway. On a bend to the left, at a short concreted section (**13min**), ignore two tracks off to the right. (The second of these is your return route.) On the few flat stretches, stop and admire the views: Aitana rising above you, the Guadalest Valley with its picturesque villages

---

Short walk: Font Molí — Guadalest Valley overlook — Font Molí. 4km/2.5mi; 1h20min. Easy climb/descent of 180m/590ft. Equipment, access as main walk. Follow the main walk for 29min, then turn right on a track. It skirts to the left of cultivation, then cuts right through the cultivation to a *casita* (43min). From here the now-grassy track winds up to the right of the house, into another, partially-cultivated valley. Take a narrow path to the left of the cultivation. It becomes a little indistinct towards the end of the cultivation: keep a couple of terraces on your left and wind to the left of a dead tree, to reach the end of the valley (49min). Now climb out of the valley; you will see your path continuing ahead. At 52min you crest the ridge, and the whole of the Guadalest Valley lies before you. Notice, up to the left, the main walk track descending towards some rocks which mark the defile we call 'Chough Gully' — this is your goal. From the edge of the ridge, follow the path slightly left and head downhill, to wind around the top terrace. At 54min you join the main walk track: pick up the notes at the 2h-point, to return to Font Molí.

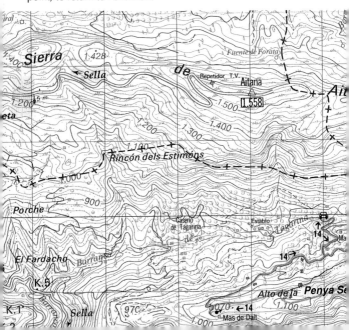

below you, and the coast at Altea in the distance.

Ignore a farm track to the right (**23min**). In **28min** your track bears right, offering the first views of Penya Mulero — there is no mistaking this huge craggy rock with its sharp pinnacles. A minute later (**29min**), ignore a track going off to the right, down into a small valley *(but turn right here for the Short walk)*. As your track bears right,

heading below the cliffs of Penya Mulero, ignore a track off left to another valley and up to the main Aitana Ridge (**35min**). In autumn, patches of white and purple heather flourish alongside the usual herbs — but be sure to look up towards the crags. Not only might you have disturbed the noisy resident ravens, but you may be lucky enough to see a golden eagle. Whether stationary, perched on the top of one of the buttresses, or in flight, its size and colour make it unmistakable. Less startling, but worth a mention, are the black redstarts that flit around the bushes, and, in winter, the small flocks of rock bunting.

A saddle with a small hillock on the right and almond groves either side marks the end of the climb (**46min**). Take a last glance back at Penya Mulero and don't be surprised if you flush partridge along the next stretch. Entering another valley, you come upon El Soliguer, a pretty *casita* not permanently inhabited but still in use (**50min**). Descend gently through groves; after summer rains take care not to tread on the delicate meadow saffron crocuses which push their way through the stony path. Confrides Castle comes into view at the top of a rise, precariously perched on top of a craggy outcrop in the northwest (**1h**).

At **1h03min** you reach a fork. You will later go down to the right, but for now go straight ahead. To your left are the antennas and domes of the military installation on top of Aitana; ahead lies another cultivated valley. Ignore tracks off into the groves; go past a chain between red gate posts (**1h18min**). The track leads down to Partagás (**1h23min**), in the setting shown on page 85.

Retrace your steps to the fork and turn left downhill (**1h43min**). As you descend through this high valley listen for the raucous calls of chough and locate them much further down as they fly in and out from the high rocks. The track sweeps round an old ruined *casita* (**1h55min**) and continues downhill with views of Aixorta ahead. The Short walk rejoins from the right (**2h**) just before the track passes between high rocks on either side (we call this narrow defile 'Chough Gully'). Look out also for blue rock thrush and for the deep *nevera* (snow well) alongside the track on the left.

Continue until you rejoin the concreted section of your outward track (**2h14min**). Turn left and retrace your steps to Font Molí, either by descending on the rough path straight down to the *font* or by continuing along the track which leads you there more gently (**2h25min**).

Map pages 86-87   **Distance:** 8km/5mi; 2h55min

Grade: moderate, with an ascent and corresponding descent of 230m/750ft. A high-altitude walk along a fairly wide ridge (avoid windy days). Despite the lack of a path, navigation is only a problem in the event of mist or low cloud.

Equipment: see page 42; also compass

How to get there and return: 🚗 At the 4.9km-point on the Sella to Puerto de Tudons road (the 23km-point on Car tour 4), turn right on a rough (but motorable) dirt road. Drive all the way up the valley, past German riding stables. Park just 5km after the turn-off from the asphalt road, in a wide open area on the left.

This walk offers splendid views and is high enough to blow away all the cobwebs. Short though it is, this is a must for those who enjoy ridge walks.

Begin by continuing up the hill on the forestry road. Pass two houses on the left and then a track on the right marked by cairns (**16min**) — your return route. The road zigzags up towards the Penya Mulero Ridge and Aitana, but you leave it at the top of a rise, where there is a *casita* above on the right and a drystone wall (**29min**). At this point the track runs straight ahead towards a *finca*, but take the sharp hairpin bend to the right, going past the *casita*. Ignore the track up left to the *casita*, but take the next one (about 20m/yds further on), heading for another house. Just before you reach it, two craggy hills appear in front of you. You are making for the saddle between them.

The track, rocky and in poor condition, goes past the house (**34min**) and then runs out at its upper terraces (**40min**). Freewheel left uphill to the saddle (**43min**). From here the mountain views are breathtaking — Aitana to the north and Campana behind El Realet (known locally

Ruined house and terraces (1h38min into the walk)

as 'the Shark's Teeth') to the south. Stretching to the west is the Penya Sella Ridge with a sheer drop to the Sella valley below. From here to the far end of the ridge there is no obvious path (so watch out for snakes!), but the walking is easy, and there is no danger of getting lost.

Turn right and climb to the first summit (**56min**). Continuing west, you'll see a couple of cairns. The second marks the second, highest peak (1106m/3630ft). From here, descend steeply over smooth rocks and then across the saddle, heading for a third 'peak'. This is in fact a rounded shoulder with twin summits, the first reached at **1h33min** and the second, across another shallow saddle, at **1h38min**. From here, you will see the ruined house shown on page 89, its terracing stretching almost to the ridge top. Make your way down to the terraces and ruins.

Take the overgrown track going left from the side of the house and soon meet another track. Turn left and head west on a continuation of the ridge. Ahead you will see an old *finca*, Mas de Dalt, a makeshift windsock indicating its use as a refuge by hang-gliders. As you approach the *finca* (**2h**), a track joins you from below on the right. You will take this track, but first explore a bit — the house, a well, and the jumping-off spot for the hang-gliders taking

the quick route down to Sella! Return to the junction and go left downhill, a sharp descent. You pass an old *era* (threshing floor) and a few houses (**2h 30min**). Meet the main forestry road of your outward route, turn left and continue down to your car (**2h55min**).

Walk 15: Aixorta rises behind the Embalse de Guadalest.

15 EMBALSE DE GUADALEST

Map pages 86-87; photograph opposite

Distance: 10km/6.2mi; 2h25min

Grade: easy, with just two short steep sections (total ascent/descent 100m/330ft). The paths are good, and you can't get lost.

Equipment: see page 42

How to get there and return: 🚌 to the 10km marker on the C3313 just east of Guadalest (the 30km-point of Car tour 3). Drive down the tree-lined road, signposted 'Embalse de Guadalest'. This takes you to the dam wall. Park in the car park.

Shorter walk: Embalse de Guadalest, south bank. 5km/3mi; 1h30min. Grade, equipment, access as above. Instead of crossing the dam wall at the start, take the track skirting the southern side of the reservoir. After 31min turn right on a track which descends quite steeply towards the river. Take the little path (44min) down to the pebbly beach at the side of the water (*P*15). Return the same way.

It is so unusual in this part of Spain to be able to walk close to water for any length of time that we felt this delightful walk should not be omitted, despite the fact that some of it is along the narrow service road around the reservoir. The reservoir is surrounded by mountains, and you will be able to appreciate their grandeur without the effort of climbing them.

Start the walk by crossing the dam. Aixorta is visible ahead (photograph opposite) and the immense gorge carved out by the Guadalest River falls away on your right. The Serrella Ridge stretches along to the left and, if you look carefully at three trees at the end of the Aixorta Ridge, you will see Serrella Castle, well camouflaged amongst the rocks. Also to the left, Benimantell Castle (or El Castellet) perches precariously on top of a rocky out-crop (from further round the reservoir it looks even more startling). Directly behind you is Guadalest Castle.

At the end of the dam wall, follow the road (marked with superfluous red dots) left along the side of the water. At times it rises above the high banks of the reservoir before falling back down again. At the far end of the reservoir you will see the village of Beniardá, the antennas on top of Aitana and Confrides Castle — another astonishing feat of construction. The road sweeps round what could, in wetter times, be arms of the reservoir but the steep banks are now clad with pines or almond groves and, in more sheltered spots, with *nísperos* (medlars) and a few vines. Added to the calls of Sardinian warblers and whinchats are the calls of the gulls on the water — an unusual sound in this mountainous terrain.

As you join a road coming in from the right (from the direction of Castell de Castells; **56min**), turn left and continue around the reservoir, sometimes in the open, sometimes through pines. Towards the end of the reservoir (**1h15min**) you begin to hear the beautiful sound of running water deep in the valley below. The source of the sound becomes evident as you reach a bridge across the sparklingly clear Guadalest River (**1h25min**). Before crossing you might like to take a detour up the side of the river just for the pleasure of watching the water running between the reeds and cascading over the rocks, with two small waterfalls nearby.

After crossing the bridge the road sweeps round to the left and climbs quite sharply, passing Beniardá's municipal swimming pool (**1h33min**). About 100m/yds past the pool, turn off left through a gatepost bearing a red dot. (The road bears right into the village where refreshment is available.) You are now on a fairly wide track leading downhill. Ignore a track to the right and continue heading down towards the river. Reach water level (**1h40min**) and continue on a path to the right, through some pines. A detour on a path going off to the left at this point takes you to the water's edge — a lovely spot for a break (**P**15).

Return to the main track alongside the river (more red dots). It crosses a little *barranco* coming down from Beniardá and passes through an area of trees and reeds. It then climbs, steeply again, to a wide track running along the southern bank of the reservoir (**1h53min**). Take this track. Notice, on the right, a couple of minutes later, a section of an enclosed *canaleta*. Further on, the holes in the steep sandy banks of the reservoir are the nests of bee-eaters. These colourful, migratory birds are unmistakable, and you are quite likely to see them in spring or summer. A leisurely stroll takes you back to your car (**2h25min**).

16 GUADALEST RIVER: CIRCUIT FROM CALLOSA D'EN SARRIA

Distance: 8.5km/5.3mi; 2h50min   **See also photograph opposite**

Grade: easy, but with a couple of steep ascents (310m/1020ft overall), and a short stretch along a *canaleta* wall. Be prepared to get your feet wet.

Equipment: see page 42

How to get there and return: 🚌 to/from Callosa d'En Sarriá (the 20km-point on Car tour 3). Park close to the old brickworks.

Alternative walk: Pont de Gines. 7km/4.3mi; 2h20min. Access, equipment, grade as main walk (but the climb is only 80m/260ft). Follow the main walk upriver to the Pont de Gines and return the same way.

This delightful river walk through a fertile valley surrounded by mountain peaks can be undertaken even in the heat of summer. Halfway along there is a bar-restaurant. On the return you climb above the valley and then descend along rural tracks back to the river. Wild flowers abound at most times of the year and cheerful birdsong will accompany you along the way.

Begin the walk by going down the narrow road past the old brickworks (ignore the 'privado' sign; this is an official PR route), descending steeply in the setting shown on page 95. The asphalt ends at a cross roads (**16min**). Turn right on a track, cross the river bed and bear right, skirting the river as it meanders along the valley. Initially the river is on your right, but you will cross it a few times. Ignore tracks off to *fincas* and groves; keep to the river track which is lined with willows and giant reeds. The lush vegetation and clear flowing water attract sandpipers and warblers, especially in the breeding season, and frogs croak noisily from the still pools. Ignore a ford going up to a market garden (**23min**) but, when the track comes to an end at the water's edge (**26min**), cross the river on stepping stones.

Now follow a farm track a little way along the right bank. When it peters out, make your way along the edge of some groves, always following the river. When it bears right (just before a *casita* with an orange-tiled roof), clamber over a couple of boulders (**33min**), to another track. Pass the access road to the *casita* and cross the river again (**38min**), just before a house with a poplar tree.

At **46min** the track runs out again, but a narrow footpath continues to the left for a further 50m/yds, before rising slightly (just opposite a red sandstone cliff) to a

Opposite: Gines, with Aixorta and Serrella in the background. It's worth taking a 10-15min detour into this hamlet: some of the houses have been well restored, especially the one alongside the old ermita.

stone water tank and *canaleta*. Walk along the narrow wall of the *canaleta* — only about 30 paces — and back onto a track. At the time of writing the *canaleta* was being gradually replaced by pipes and may eventually disappear. Walk alongside the pipes which have already been laid and reach a water control gate (**49min**).

Here keep ahead on a rough track; Guadalest Castle is perched on the pinnacle ahead. The track fords the river again and continues left to another ford below a grand old four-storey *finca* (**50min**). At **55min** the path takes you through a narrow defile where another water control station has been built. Clamber up and round it, then back down to the track. Continue for about 100m/yds, ford the river again on stepping stones, and join a track running along the right bank (**1h04min**). The next ford, with a plank to assist you, takes you back to the left bank. A few minutes later the bar-restaurant El Riu comes into view on the Pont de Gines, the road bridge across the river. Go under the bridge (**1h11min**), then turn left up to the road. *(From here the Alternative walk returns the same way.)*

Walking towards the bridge from the point where you came out on to the road, turn right up a narrow, poorly-surfaced asphalt road. Wind steeply above the valley; some pines providing welcome shade on the climb. At **1h33min** pass the access road to Gines, the little settlement shown on page 92. It's worth a detour. But the main walk continues up the road. Before reaching the highest point, turn left on an initially-unsurfaced road (opposite a walkers' signpost; **1h43min**).

A few minutes along, at a junction just past a house, take the yellow and white PR-marked route straight ahead through almond terraces. As you round a bend, Callosa comes into view through a gap in the hills, the Bernia Ridge rising behind it. Ignore minor tracks on the left but, on a sharp bend, take the waymarked track going left (**1h54min**). Keep to this main track, rounding the head of a *barranco*, with good views of all the interesting rock formations in the area. Low pines line the route. Beside a *casita*, you pass a signpost to the farm of Ferraget, before winding down to the river bed (**2h21min**) and your outward route. Turn right, cross the river (**2h28min**) and turn left on the asphalt road for the steep climb back to the brickworks at Callosa (**2h50min**).

At the start of the walk, you pass through a fertile area of medlar and lemon groves with Campana, Ponoch and the Sierra de Aitana ahead.

17 CAMÍ DE L'ESCALETA: FROM BOCAIRENT TO POU CLAR

See also cover photograph and photograph page 33

Distance: 6km/3.7mi; 1h50min

Grade: easy descent of 300m/980ft; no navigation problems.

Equipment: see page 42

How to get there: 🚗 to Bocairent (the 89km-point on Car tour 4). Park in the old square (follow signs to the Tourist Information Office).
To return: 🚌 from Pou Clar to Bocairent (the infrequent service passes just a few minutes after leaving Ontinyent; check times in advance). Or retrace your steps (add 1h50min).

Short walk: Covetes de los Moros. See description page 98.

T he Camí de l'Escaleta is the old mule trail which served the textile factories *(fabricas)* strung out along the Barranco de Ontiniente from Bocairent to Ontinyent. The waters of the *barranco* were used in the preparation of textiles, and mules carried finished bales to the towns. Pou Clar, a lovely *font* with deep pools and picnic tables, is a picturesque end to this gentle and delightful trail.

Start out at the Tourist Office. Walk up the hill on the medieval cobbled road to the old bridge across the *barranco* (**6min**; photograph page 33). The road sweeps left, passing the village *lavadero* (**10min**) and a *font,* before coming to a collection of houses and a cross, at a junction

(**19min**). Take the middle, asphalted road; it soon peters out into a stony track — the beginning of the Camí de l'Escaleta. It disappears for a while as you cross roadworks, but you can see it continuing on the other side.

After a few minutes look left for your route — up a series of little steps hewn out of the rock. Deeply pitted from the constant pounding of hooves, the trail takes you almost parallel with a track, then over the side of the hill, to another track. Cross this and locate the continuation of your trail as it descends into the Barranco de la Luna. At **56min**, after the first 'bobsleigh' section (shown below), the Barranco de Ontiniente comes in from the left and the first old *fabrica* comes into sight (see cover photograph). The trail bears left, down to the old building, and continues along the *barranco* to a second *fabrica* (**1h04min**), from where it widens to a track. High cliffs, pitted with caves, rise up out of the *barranco,* and terraces adorn the gentler slopes. The *barranco* has been dammed in places near the mills, and deciduous trees line its floor, which you will criss-cross at times.

When the track forks go left on a path to the third *fabrica* (**1h06min**). Villa Flor, the largest of the mills, is about 100m/330ft long (**1h15min**). Not far beyond it, a disused *canaleta* winds past the fifth *fabrica* (**1h24min**). The trail goes under the *canaleta* and skirts the fence of a house (**1h31min**), before joining its access track. Turn left, pass a hydroelectric plant and reach the main Bocairent/Ontinyent road (**1h40min**). Turn left. Just after a turn-off left to Fontaneta, Pou Clar lies below on your left (**1h50min**). Flag down your bus at the Fontaneta junction.

The walk follows an old mule trail, the Camí de l'Escaleta. At times it is stony or well-packed earth, but there are some amazing sections cut from the solid rock — resembling bobsleigh runs! Here are some walkers on the first 'bobsleigh run'. See also cover photograph, which shows the approach to the first textile mill.

Covetes de los Moros: see Short walk below.

Short walk: Covetes de los Moros. 2km/1.2mi; 35min. Easy. Access and equipment as main walk. This stroll explores the network of 53 caves shown above. Hewn out of the cliff, they were once inhabited, probably by the Moors. While you can go directly there and back (signposted from the Tourist Office; 25min return), try this more pleasant, circular route. Follow the main walk to the bridge (6min). A couple of minutes later, before reaching the *lavadero*, take an obvious path going steeply down to the left. Cross a stream and bear left. The path runs above a couple of caves and descends, to skirt the right bank of the stream all the way to the *covetes*. Metal steps take you up the vertical cliff to the only entrance. After your visit, return to the stream and turn right. Cross the stream just below its junction with a second stream, then strike uphill to the top of a rise. Ahead is the first Station of the Cross leading to a hilltop *ermita*. Make for this but, when you get there, turn left down a wide path. Cross an old bridge and follow a path to a cobbled road, where you turn left and climb back up to the main square (35min).

18 ALCOI • BARRANC DEL SINC • COLL SABATA • MONTCABRER • RACO LLOBET • MURO DE ALCOI

Distance: 20km/12.4mi; 5h40min   **See also photograph opposite**

Grade: strenuous, with ascents of 770m/2520ft and descents of 870m/2850ft. Mostly on good tracks and paths; navigation straightforward.

Equipment: see page 42; also compass, long trousers, plenty of water

How to get there: 🚌 to the Alcoyana bus station in Alcoi. Turn right along Avinguda l'Alameda (the main road just up from the bus station). Just before a bridge and the tall Alcoy Plaza building (5min), you reach the Mercadona supermarket, where the walk begins. Or 🚗 to Alcoi (the 55km-point on Car tour 4 (page 31). From the Mercadona supermarket (58km), use the *walking* notes on page 101, to park near the brickworks. *To return:* 🚌 from Muro to the first stop past Alcoi's railway station

Short walk: Barranc del Sinc. 2km/1.2mi; 40min. Easy stroll. Access: 🚗 to/from Alcoi (see instructions for motorists above). Follow the main walk from the 25min-point to the 44min-point, then retrace your steps.

Alternative walk (just one of many possible alternatives in the Sierra de Mariola, where you can link up Walks 18-20): Alcoi — Coll Sabata — Cocentaina. 13km/8mi; 4h20min. Moderate-strenuous, with a climb of 440m/1440ft and a descent of 360m/1180ft. Equipment as main walk, less long trousers. Access as main walk; return by 🚌 from Cocentaina, and walk back to the Alcoyana bus station or your car. Follow the main walk to Coll Sabata (2h). From here you will follow a well-waymarked route down to Cocentaina. Take the path straight ahead, signposted 'Refugio las Foietes'. This leads over the Talecó de D'Alt, a high cliff above the Barranco de Capenal. After a short steep drop, it joins an overgrown track, where you turn right (2h30min) and pass a small house. The track narrows to a path and passes through an area of fire-damaged woodland, before joining another track (2h43min). Turn left towards a quarry on the hillside ahead. At a junction (2h52min) take the wide track left to 'Castell', 'Sant Cristófol'. (The Refugio las Foietes, a shelter with water and picnic benches, is off to the *right*. On week-ends and *fiestas* in season, when it is open, you would have access to the toilets and other indoor facilities.) Fork right at the next junction and descend towards the cliffs. Cross the asphalted quarry road (2h58min) and head downhill on a track, watching for a 'Castell' signpost, indicating your ongoing path to the left. (The track descends to Cocentaina's railway station.) The path passes above a grand old *finca*, Mas de la Penya, then comes to a delightful spot directly under the *penya* itself — a massive cliff much used by Alcoi's rock-climbing fraternity (3h 08min; *P*18c). The path continues to a narrow asphalt road (3h21min). Turn left uphill, past a chain barrier, to reach a crest overlooking Cocentaina Castle. From here take the path going down to the left, to the castle *mirador* (3h34min). Now a concrete road leads you steeply down to Sant Cristófol — an extensive *zona recreativa* just above Cocentaina, with a bar-restaurant (3h55min; *P*18b). Continue down the road for a few minutes, then turn right on a narrow PR-waymarked path. It crosses the railway line, runs above the industrial area, crosses a track and descends to an asphalt road. Turn right and make for the church. Cross the church square diagonally, then turn right up Carrer Major, a pedestrian precinct. At the top, turn left and left again to reach Plaza Alcalde Reig (4h20min), from where you can catch the bus back to Alcoi.

Opposite: Snow on Montcabrer (Walk 18)

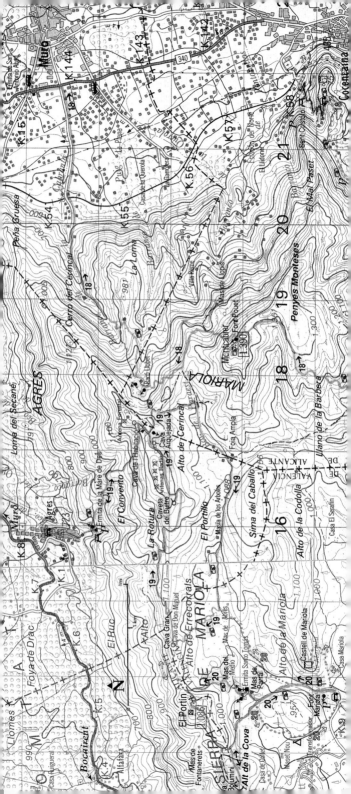

The Barranc del Sinc provides a picturesque start to this walk, which takes you over Coll Sabata and across rocky ridges to the summit of Montcabrer (1390m/4560ft). It then descends into the cultivated valley of Racó Llobet and follows another *barranco* down into Muro. It is a delightful walk offering a variety of landscape and views.

Start out at the Mercadona supermarket. From its front door, cross Avinguda l'Alameda and go up Carrer Isaac Peral. This road leads directly uphill into Calle La Salle and then Carrer Barranc del Sinc. Pass a *font* and the municipal swimming pool on the right, then an electricity station on the left. Continue past the last row of houses to a brickworks (its chimney is visible ahead; **25min**). Those travelling by car should park near here, and deduct 25min from all times given below. Take the track which heads right, on the bend, at the brickworks. From here you are looking directly at the cliffs shown opposite — the entrance to the Barranc del Sinc. You will see your track winding towards it. The red and white GR7 markers, sometimes faded, will take you all the way to the top of Montcabrer. The track crosses the *barranco* and leads you through the defile and to a path. At about **33min** you come upon a beautiful picnic spot (*P*18a), where the roughly-cobbled path and steps pass close to the water-course. There will not always be water here, but even when dry it is an impressive spot. Cliffs tower above as the path continues along the *barranco*, crossing from side to side, passing a *casita* with a willow tree (**44min**). *(The Short walk turns back here.)* Now you leave the *barranco* bed, continuing at a higher level through pines which are home to short-toed treecreepers. Ignore a track to the left (**53min**) and continue parallel with the *barranco,* until a steep climb takes you past a water control station ('C Motor' on the map; **1h05min**) to an asphalt road. Turn left. Being a cul-de-sac, the road carries little traffic.

The *barranco* deepens on your left as you climb steeply, eventually passing a large storage building just before Mas Nou, a little community with one very old house and some new ones (**1h25min**). The road continues round into Alcoi, but you must take the track which goes up to the right, just on the bend. This takes you away from the Barranc del Sinc and up through a pine wood, past a chain barrier, to Mas de Capellá and its surrounding terraces (**1h40min**). Pass between the main buildings and turn right to ascend gently through fruit and almond groves and past a couple of sheds. As the track sweeps right (**1h51min**) take the waymarked path to the left and climb through a valley of pine trees to a clearing — Coll Sabata (**2h**). Look out around here for Dartford warblers, which are resident on these upper slopes. A track and several paths leave from the col. *(For the Alternative walk, take the path straight ahead.)*

The main walk takes the path up to the left, past an enclosure containing an antenna. Ignore a signposted path to the left (**2h08min**), and fork right uphill over pine-clad slopes where, in autumn, the heather is quite spectacular. Looking back once past the tree line (**2h20min**), you will see Alcoi spread out in the valley below, with the heavily-wooded slopes and *ermita* of Font Roja across to the right. As the path approaches and crosses a *lomo*, or shoulder, it becomes quite indistinct on the rocky terrain, especially in snow. However it is clearly marked with very large cairns and GR7 markers. The walking is easy, and the cairns lead you to a small crest (**2h49min**), where a deep *barranco* goes down left towards Font Mariola. In good weather you may find it hard to believe that we had to wade through knee-deep snow here one February — but the photograph on page 98 proves it!

From the crest, look for your continuing path making its way round towards the rocky outcrop of Penyes Monteses, which has a little pole on top. The path is clear for a while and gradually loses altitude. As it drops over the rocks to a lower level, it becomes indistinct for a short time. Keep about 20m/65ft below the highest point of the ridge and look carefully for the rather faded GR7 markers. The path soon reappears and leads you round to the left of Penyes Monteses (**2h55min**). From there the path is almost level and takes you round to Montcabrer (you can see the craggy summit ahead). At the end of the open stretch (**3h03min**) the crags are directly ahead and, as the

The walker is a mere dot in the landscape, below the impressive cliffs which flank the narrow entrance to the Barranc del Sinc (Picnic 18a).

path winds round them to the right, you should leave it: take the little path up left to the summit (**3h13min**). On returning to the main path, turn left to reach a terrace directly under the end of the crags. This is Font Pouet, where you will find a walkers' notice asking you to observe the country code (**3h25min**).

Continue on this path, descending at first gradually and then more steeply. Ignore a turn-off right to Mas de Llopis (**3h38min**) and reach a saddle (**3h44min**) at the top of the slopes above Muro. From here the GR7 goes left towards Font Mariola, but you should ignore this and turn right downhill on a path just a few metres/yards further on. You wind down quite steeply through prickly gorse, before contouring above cultivated terraces and getting your first glimpse of the house at Racó Llobet as you round a bend. The path circles above its terraces, then decends to a track (**4h**). Turn left, pass the dry Fuente de Vicente, and reach the house (**4h04min**). Although not inhabited, it has been restored and retains much of its original character.

Walk to the right of the house on a narrow but clear path which winds right and then left, to a track. Turn right on the track but, almost immediately, turn right again, on a narrow path which runs above the broad terraces and leads to the Barranco de Puig. Follow the left bank of this beautiful *barranco* through thick vegetation, with Serrella dominating the view ahead, to a ruined farm (**4h25min**). Turn left at the track here; about 100m/yds further on you meet the track coming down from Racó. Turn sharp right and continue downhill to a right-hand bend, just past a huge boulder (**4h35min**). Here take the path on the left. (Both track and path follow the Barranco de la Cabrantá, but the path is more pleasant.) Just after passing a *casita* (**4h43min**), rejoin the track as it comes in from the right.

At about **5h05min** you pass the first houses on the out-skirts of Muro. Cross the railway and continue straight on to the main road (**5h33min**). Turn left towards the petrol station (200m/yds away; adjacent bars, café, restaurant), then cross the road to a roundabout where there are two more restaurants. Turn right at the roundabout towards Muro centre. Catch your bus a few metres/yards along on the left outside a shop, Murelec Electricidad (**5h40min**; no sign, but the bus is used to picking up here). Back in Alcoi, alight from the bus at the stop *after* the railway station, then walk down the hill to Avinguda l'Alameda and back to the Alcoyana bus station. Or use the notes at the start of the walk to return to your car (add 25min).

19 THE *CAVAS:* CIRCUIT FROM AGRES

See map pages 100-101; see also photograph and notes pages 6-7
Distance: 13.5km/8.4mi; 5h08min

Grade: fairly strenuous, with ascents and corresponding descents of 820m/2700ft overall. The paths and tracks are good underfoot, except one short section along the ridge, where the path crosses rocks and is indistinct. Navigation is straightforward.

Equipment: see page 42; also compass

How to get there and return: 🚌 to/from Agres (the 77km-point on Car tour 4). Park in the village and make your way to the church. Note: It is possible to shorten the walk by 2h, and cut out about 600m/1970ft of climb and descent. by driving up to the refuge and starting there. Drive up the road towards the *ermita,* but then turn right opposite the third Station of the Cross. ***But be warned!*** This road, although reasonably wide and well-surfaced, *is extremely steep with hairpins as sharp as hairpins can get and its sides are unprotected from treacherous drops.*

Shorter walk: Agres — three *cavas* — Agres. 7.5km/4.7mi; 3h. Fairly strenuous, with ascents/corresponding descents totalling 650m/2130ft. Access as above; equipment as page 42. This out and back hike takes in three of the four snow wells visited on the main walk. Follow the main walk to the Cava de l'Habitació (1h15min). Then return to the refuge and continue along the road to Cava Arquejada, which you can see ahead. Take the road which continues behind this *cava.* In 10 minutes, as it turns slightly left and starts to descend, take a track off to the right, which leads into the small depression housing Caveta del Buitre (1h32min). Retrace your steps all the way back to Agres.

Alternatives: This walk and Walks 18 and 20 inter-connect, so a variety of alternative routes can easily be devised.

This walk takes you up pine-clad mountain slopes, down into a peaceful, sheltered valley with a large working farm, and along a ridge with amazing views on either side. *And* there are buildings to explore. In addition to an *ermita* and a *refugio* (mountain hut), we pass four *cavas* (snow wells; see pages 6-7), probably all dating from the 17th century. Such wells were only built in exposed areas, where snowfall was virtually guaranteed — so, even on a sunny day, remember that it could be very windy and somewhat chilly up on this high sierra.

Start out by going up the road to the left of the church (as you face it). Pass a *font* on the left and look for the Ermita de la Mare de Deu, your first objective, on the hill ahead. Just after a small playground on the outskirts of Agres (**4min**), climb stone steps on the right. At the top, join the road to the *ermita* at the second Station of the Cross. Turn left uphill, pass the tortuous road up to the refuge, and reach the *ermita* in **11min** (*P*19). Take the narrow concrete road to the left, in front of the buildings, through the car park. Pass a *font* and take the track straight ahead, behind a chain barrier.

The track climbs quite steeply, providing views down

Cava Arquejada, sited at 1220m/ 4000ft, near the refuge, it is elegantly constructed with six gothic arches topping the hexagonal exterior.

into the Agres valley. Close to the ruins of the old convent building, small signs ('Cocentaina' and 'Cava') direct you onto a path going right (**15min**). Ignore the yellow and white waymarked path to the left (**19min**) and continue straight ahead through pines, alongside a *barranco*. You cross this stream (**25min**) just before a path comes in on the left. There are many hunters' paths and short-cuts, but you will have no difficulty keeping to the clear, zigzagging, main path. As you progress uphill you will see two groups of antennas on the ridge ahead. You are making for the refuge which is between them. At **57min** meet a wide track. Ignore signs directing you to the right (to the refuge); cross the track diagonally to the left continuing uphill on a rocky footpath with yellow and white waymarks. Shortly after a pebbly stretch of path, the refuge appears just above you (**1h10min**). This refuge (open and manned at weekends and holidays) was built in 1974 on the site of a ruined house, previously occupied by the workers and guardians of the wells. Walk about 100m/yds to the left on the vehicle access road, to look at the Cava de l'Habitació — 7m/23ft in diameter and 10m/33ft deep, with a semicircular crypt roof. Leave this well (**1h15min**) and return to the refuge: another *cava* is just beyond it — visited on the return route.

Just opposite the refuge, take the track waymarked in red, going left towards the craggy summit of Montcabrer. Pass a large water tank on the right (**1h18min**) and reach an open area with a steep drop ahead. The track winds to the left and forks. Take the right fork, going slightly downhill. The track then bears right, and the amphitheatre of Racó Llobet opens up below on the left (**1h21min**). The path going straight ahead leads to the summit of Montcabrer (Walk 18), but your track goes down to the right, into the cultivated valley. It soon narrows into a path and passes some terraces on the right, before reverting to a track and zigzagging down into the valley. On this stretch you meet a path coming in from the left (**1h33min**) and pick up the red and white way-

marks of the GR7. Almost immediately, ignore a path
going left to some terraces. Your track, now grassy and
pleasant, passes through pines and alongside a *barranco*.
At **1h40min** you reach a high metal fence. Walk alongside the fence, through a cultivated area, to the large farm
complex of Foia Ampla (**1h50min**). If any of their big noisy
black dogs are loose, just slow down, let them have a sniff
and gradually make your way past. Go up the now-wide
track, leaving the main buildings on your left. You rise
slightly to a signposted junction (**1h53min**). The track to
the right leads back to the refuge, but go straight ahead,
following the red and white waymarks. In a few minutes,
as you round a bend, look up to the top of the ridge ahead
and to the right, to locate the circular stone building of
the Cava Gran — your next port of call.

Continue along the track past a modern house on the
right, with a colourful well (**2h08min**). You will see an
old *finca* set into the hillside ahead, below the crags of
El Portín and the *cava* (**2h11min**). Six minutes past this
view you must turn off to the right. To find this turn-off,
locate another *finca*, Mas de Abres, up on the left amongst
pines. When you are level with it, a drystone wall and
two adjacent pine trees, each carrying red and white GR7
waymarks, will be on your left. To the *right,* about 20m/
yds *before* these trees, is the path you want (**2h17min**):
you will see it snaking up towards the *cava,* which itself
is not visible from this point. (*Alternative walk 20 joins
here.*) There are no waymarks from now on.

The path crosses a *barranco* and passes old terraces
and ploughed fields before heading uphill. It is well trod-
den, mainly by hunters. As you gain height you have a
view left over ploughed fields to the Castillo de Mariola
(Short walk 20-2) perched on top of a rocky ridge. The
path climbs steeply through patches of Valencian oaks to
Cava Gran (sometimes called Cava de Don Miguel;
2h40min). This huge snow well, sited at 1060m/3475ft,
looks more like a fortress — so thick are its walls. It is
hexagonal, constructed on two levels, and with three
tunnels. Ruins of the workers' building are close by.

With your back to the main tunnel, go straight ahead,
heading east along the ridge (over several small peaks),
to make for the next *cava*. (*The path heading west along
the ridge at this point would take you to El Portín in 12
minutes, where you could join Walk 20.*) The terrain is
rocky, and the path is indistinct in places. There are
various different routes over the rocks, but if you stay just

below and on the right-hand (southern) side of the ridge, you will pick up the main path from time to time. At **3h14min** you come to a small saddle from where you have a good view into the valley below. The peak ahead is stepped with rectangular rocks, and the dense undergrowth on the south side is impassable. So climb the few metres/yards to the top of the saddle, and you will see a track coming up through the pine forest below on the northern side. Descend the few metres to the track and turn right, to round the 'stepped' peak and climb back to the top of the ridge (**3h28min**). Then leave the track just before it begins to descend, and take a path on the left; it continues east along the ridge.

Maintain altitude atop the ridge until you meet a wide track (which has come up from Font Mariola; **3h36min**). Turn left uphill here. After about 50m/yds, go left on another track, into a depression which houses the Caveta del Buitre ('Vulture's Well'; photograph page 7). This well has four access points, and its circular cupola is in excellent condition. Return to the track and continue to the Cava Arquejada (**3h53min**; photograph page 106). It is probably the most beautiful and most visited *nevera* in Alicante. The well itself is fashioned mainly from natural rock and has six upper openings and one lower tunnel opening. From here head back to the refuge (**3h58min**).

To return to Agres, retrace your outward path from below the refuge. Cross the wide track (**4h13min**) and zigzag downhill, ignoring tracks off to the right, until you reach the signposted junction (**4h51min**). Turn left and walk in front of the *ermita* (**4h57min**). Take the road downhill as far as the second Station, where steps off to the right lead you back into Agres (**5h08min**).

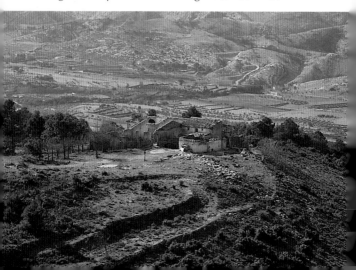

20 FONT MARIOLA • ERMITA DE SAN TOMAS • EL PORTIN • ALT DE LA COVA • COVA DE BOLUMINI • FONT MARIOLA

See map pages 100-101 and photograph opposite

Distance: 8km/5mi; 2h25min

Grade: quite easy, with a gentle ascent of 220m/720ft to the main ridge at El Portín and corresponding descent. Paths are generally good, but overgrown in places — care is needed to locate them.

Equipment: see page 42; also compass, long trousers

How to get there and return: 🚌 to Font Mariola (the 100km-point on Car tour 4). Park in the picnic/camping area.

Short walks (both are easy; access as above; equipment as page 42)

1   Font Mariola circuit. 2.8km/1.7mi; 50min. Follow the main walk to the turn off just before the *ermita* (19min). Turn left, and immediately left again, to walk along the edge of the pine wood and the ploughed field to the campsite visible ahead. Turn left on the asphalt road, and follow it back to Font Mariola (red and white GR7 waymarks).

2   Mariola Castle. 1.6km/1mi; 50min. From the picnic benches at Font Mariola you can see the Moorish castle atop the heavily-wooded hill. Walk up the track (a post on the left is marked with red paint), into the pines. The track becomes a path, for a while following the boundary fence of a *finca* down to the right. After a few minutes it bears left up the hill and leads you to the ruins of the castle. Return the same way.

Alternative walk: The main walk connects with the other two walks in the Sierra de Mariola (Walks 18 and 19), so many alternatives can be devised; this is just one possibility: Font Mariola — Cava Gran — El Portín — Font Mariola. 9km/5.6mi; 2h45min. Grade, access, equipment as main walk (long trousers not needed). Follow the main walk to the crossroads at 10min. Go straight ahead on the track with GR7 waymarks, towards Foia Ampla. But at about 35min, when the large Mas de Abres *finca* is just above you on the right, take the faint path down to the left. This is the path to Cava Gran. Pick up the notes for Walk 19 at the 2h17min-point (page 107). After visiting Cava Gran, take the path running west along the ridge, to the saddle below El Portín. Here you rejoin the main walk at the 50min-point; follow it to the end.

This delightful walk leads you through the fertile, well-wooded Mariola valley and up onto a sheer ridge overlooking the valley of Agres. You'll clamber up onto the crags at the top of the ridge and walk through some prickly gorse (don't forget the long trousers!) to the site of an early Iberian settlement. Just over the rocky shelf, you explore a massive cave near the sheer cliff face, before descending back into the valley. Font Mariola is an idyllic place to relax and picnic (*P*20) — as long as it is during the week and out of season! You could easily combine this walk with Short walk 2 up to the castle.

   The walk starts at the picnic benches by the *font*. Mariola Castle is perched on the knoll on the right, and

Opposite: the Mas de Fontanerets from El Portín, with the Agres valley in the background

your track runs below it, heading up the valley through mature pine woods. At a crossroads (**10min**) turn onto a wide but rough track going left over a low bridge. *(But for the Alternative walk, keep straight ahead on the main track.)* At **19min** a track coming in from the left is your return route. *(Short walk 1 turns left here.)* Continue as the track sweeps round to the right towards some buildings — Mas de Parral and the Ermita de San Tomás (**23min**). Mas de Parral was once a magnificent *finca* and is presently being restored. As you approach you may be greeted noisily by a pack of small dogs. They are curious, not dangerous, so let them have a sniff before you disentangle yourself and turn left up the hill, past the *ermita* and towards a second farmhouse about 100m/yds away.

Just before reaching this building, locate a well alongside a wide track on the right. Look on the terrace above the well, for a small path climbing up another terrace towards the sierra. Climb above the well and follow this path as it maintains almost constant altitude, passing through the terraces and then pines. Maintain your direction as you cross a rough track (**28min**), *and keep on the narrow path however indistinct it may seem.* It soon leads to a wire fence surrounding the fields belonging to Mas del Medio, which comes into view across the fields. The path follows the fence for a few minutes, before leaving it and rising about 10m/yds to the left across a loose and rocky surface. You climb to a low crest (**34min**).

This is a good spot to take your bearings. To the right (east) is Mas de Abres with Montcabrer rising behind it. The ridge with the *cavas* (Walk 19) stretches east to north from Mas de Abres, and your next objective — the crags of El Portín — are just ahead of you to the northwest. Follow the path as it drops into a small depression and then climbs up through thickets of gorse to a small saddle below El Portín (**50min**). *(To link up with Walk 19, head right on the path running along the top of the ridge; it will lead you, in some 12 minutes, to Cava Gran. The path is indistinct in places, but you can't get lost if you keep to the top of the ridge heading generally east.)* The main walk turns left here, climbing up towards the crags of El Portín. The path leads under the highest rocks, on the southern side, before winding round to where a short scramble will take you to the summit (**59min**).

Looking northwest you will see a rusty, large TV antenna with a fence around it, close by on a spur of the ridge. Make for this. Then, from the gate in the fence, locate the *finca* of Mas de Fontanerets in the high valley below you. Beyond that, the continuation of the ridge is Alt de la Cova, a terraced hill which is the site of an Iberian settlement. It is your next objective. From the gate you can just about make out your path running through the thick vegetation on the far side of the dip.

Without losing altitude, head south for about 100m/yds. You meet this narrow but clear path at the beginning of some old terraces. It descends, going below the lowest terrace, and takes you through sometimes prickly undergrowth, to a track (**1h10min**). To the right is the *finca* shown on page 108, Mas de Fontanerets, but you must turn left and follow the path to the saddle below Alt de la Cova (**1h18min**). From here several different paths climb the short distance, through abandoned terraces, to the plateau. Take your pick and reach Alt de la Cova in **1h30min**. The settlement dates back to the fourth to first centuries BC, and clear signs of it still remain. Local museums house many artefacts from the site, and the whole plateau is worth investigating. Evidence of past cultivation abounds, and the plateau is so strategically sited that it is easy to see why it was chosen as a site by these Bronze Age inhabitants. In the middle of the plateau there is a small depression, about 10m/30ft deep. The northern (right-hand) edge of this depression is edged with a rocky shelf. Near the far end of the shelf you will see a path going diagonally downhill to the east (everywhere else there is a sheer drop to the Agres valley below). This easy path, shielded from the drop by rocky plates, leads in a few minutes to the massive Cova de Bolumini. This cave also formed an important part of the settlement.

The path does continue past the cave, under the cliff walls and above a sheer drop, to the Fontanerets track. But rainfall in this area is relatively high, and the combination of damp rocks and slippery grass means that great care must be taken. The more cautious (including us!) will prefer to retrace their steps up to Alt de la Cova and return to the main track at the saddle (**1h50min**). Turn right and continue down towards Font Mariola. The track descends above ploughed fields, with the commercial campsite (where there is a bar/restaurant) off to the right. The *ermita* and Mas de Parral look magnificent down in the valley to your left. The track descends between fields, returning you to the track of your outward route. Turn right and enjoy a good view of Mariola Castle as you walk past the camping areas, back to your car (**2h25min**).

21 PARQUE NATURAL DE FONT ROJA

Distance: 15km/9.3mi; 4h45min

Grade: moderate, with ascents and corresponding descents totalling 800m/2620ft; tracks are good, and navigation is no problem.

Equipment: see page 42; also warm clothing, compass (in case of mist)

How to get there and return: 🚌 to/from Ibi. Alight at the stop on the slip road off the main road in the town centre; this stop is after the traffic lights, where the Centro Optico is on the right. (The stop for your return bus is just opposite.) Cross the road, go back the way the bus came in for about 30m/yds, then turn right. Pass the market and, in 'bank square' (100m/yds further on), take the second exit on the right. A five-minute walk up the hill leads to the main street, with the church to the left. Turn right; the *ayuntamiento* (town hall, with flags outside), is 100m/yds away. Or 🚗: park at the *ayuntamiento* (town hall; the 125km-point on Car tour 4).

Short walk: Ibi — Cava Canyo — Ibi. 10km/6.2mi; 2h54min. Moderate, with a climb and corresponding descent of 500m/1640ft. Equipment as page 42; access as above. Follow the end of the main walk in reverse to Masía del Canyo and Cava Canyo; return the same way.

Alternative walk: Ibi — Casa Foiaderetes — Barranco de las Zorras — Ibi. 12km/7.4mi; 3h30min. Moderate climbs/descents of 550m/1800ft. Access and equipment as main walk (no compass required). Follow the main walk to Casa Foiaderetes (59min), then take the track to the right. It winds down past terracing, lusciously green in spring, to a *finca* near the Barranco de las Zorras (Vixens' Gully; 1h15min). As the track begins to climb again, it makes a sharp right-hand bend. Leave it here, on the obvious path which goes straight ahead (1h20min). It follows the *barranco* to a four-way junction (1h50min). This is the 3h08min-point in the main walk. Turn right, and follow the main walk back to Ibi.

I n the 60s and 70s the area around Font Roja was scheduled for extensive development but, fortunately, these plans were abandoned through lack of finance. However, it was not until 1987 that environmentalists succeeded in having it declared a Parque Natural. The ecological importance of its mixed woodland and resulting ecosystem will become increasingly evident as you walk through the park. You will also pass several old *fincas* — of some importance in their time, but now abandoned. At the Font Roja complex (*P*21) you can rest and picnic in beautiful surroundings or refresh yourself at the bar-restaurant (closed Mondays) before undertaking the ascent to Menejador. As you begin to feel a bit chilly or as your legs start flagging as you climb, console yourself with the thought that you are attaining a height just greater than that of Ben Nevis. The return route takes you past three of the park's *cavas* (snow wells), before descending back into Ibi on a delightful old mule trail.

Start out with your back to the *ayuntamiento:* walk up the street opposite (Calle de Santa Lucia, but not signposted at this end). You are making for the hills you can

Font Roja (Picnic 21). This walk takes you through its mixed woodland. Above 900m/3000ft the holm (or evergreen) oak, with its dark green foliage, dominates, but the humid north-facing slopes also provide ideal conditions for other species — Valencian oak, ash, and maple. Lower down, the oaks share the land with pine, deciduous trees and shrubs whose leaves, throughout the autumn, provide colourful relief from the monotony of the evergreens. In the past, the yew tree was also present in great numbers, but today only about forty of this species remain.

see at the end of the street. On your left is the more easterly of Ibi's twin hills, this one crowned by the Ermita de Santa Lucia. Notice some steps going up on your right — your return route. *(The Short walk climbs up here.)* Almost at the edge of town you pass to the right of the Sociedad de Palomas Deportivas (Pigeon Fanciers' Club), with its array of coloured launching boxes. Just before the road sweeps round to the left (**10min**), take the track straight ahead, between two brick gate-posts. Here you pick up your first yellow and white waymarks. Almost immediately, the track turns left, to cross a small *barranco* and climb steeply up the far side. At the top, cross a track and continue straight ahead uphill, towards a small water control building ('Casa Motor' on the map) and three pines.

The track passes to the right of the building and goes round the head of the *barranco*, taking you to the foot of a steep rocky slope. The path up over the rocks is a bit of a clamber, but it is clearly marked and not difficult. As you reach each waymark, look for the next one above you, so as not to lose the route. On reaching the top of this section (**29min**), you come upon a lone pine tree and can see the continuing path going straight ahead.

The next section climbs less steeply and takes you through herbs and gorse. Take time to turn and look behind you where, from left to right, you will see Carrasqueta, Penya Roja and the Sierra de Maigmó (Walks 23-25), with the coast and *salinas* between them. At **45min**

113

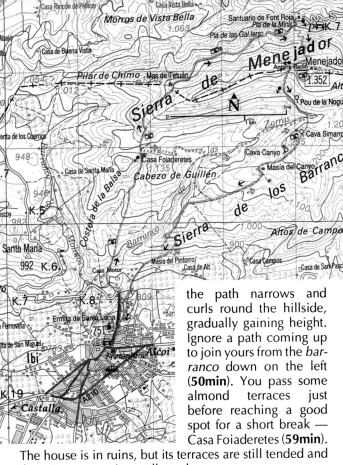

the path narrows and curls round the hillside, gradually gaining height. Ignore a path coming up to join yours from the *barranco* down on the left (**50min**). You pass some almond terraces just before reaching a good spot for a short break — Casa Foiaderetes (**59min**). The house is in ruins, but its terraces are still tended and there is an attractive well nearby.

As you leave the house a track crosses your path. Keep straight ahead. *(But the Alternative walk turns right here.)* When the path forks at the end of the almond groves, go left. In addition to yellow and white waymarks, you now pick up the red and white waymarks of the GR7, one of Spain's long distance footpaths (a similar mark is visible on the stone wall in the photograph on page 113). Take the right fork at the next junction and admire the wide-reaching views to your left — all the way across to the Sierra de Maigmó, with Biar and Villena beyond it. As you walk through this lovely area of mixed woodland, ignore another path to the right (**1h10min**; white waymarks). Pass the terraces of Mas de Tetuán and then the house itself (**1h24min**). Yew trees still stand beside its old *era* (circular threshing area).

Walk in front of the house and turn left at the junction with a track. This is a park track, and will take you to Font

Roja. Descend, quite steeply in places, past a fire watchtower on a rise to the left (**1h38min**) — an excellent place for a view down into the valley and up the heavily-wooded slopes of Menejador. Continue straight on at the junction at Pla de las Gal.lers (**1h45min**) — so named because the *gal.ler* (Valencian oak) is so abundant here. As you approach Font Roja, look well over to the left, where Montcabrer (Walk 18) rises imposingly. At Pla de la Mina (**1h54min**), the little path off to the right is your eventual route up to the summit of Menejador; but, for the moment, keep straight ahead: go down the steps through the picnic/barbecue area at the upper end of the Font Roja complex. The bar-restaurant and information centre are then just off to the left (**2h**). Further down are the large Santuario de la Virgen de los Lirios, toilets, and another picnic/camping area with views to Alcoi and Montcabrer.

From here retrace your steps to Pla de la Mina and turn left up the stepped path (signposted 'Senda Menejador') which climbs steeply to meet another park track. Turn right to a saddle (**2h30min**) just below the summit of Menejador. Here there is a junction of tracks and a large green water tank. Do the round trip (little more than 10min): walk up the path, past the building and the antenna, to the summit (1352m/4430ft). (If you want to conquer another summit, a path leads eastwards to Alto del Ginebra, about 10min away.) On your return, take the track past the water tank, but turn left immediately (**2h43min**) on a path which is designated a PR but bears only two waymarks on its whole length! It descends steeply past an old stone well (**2h53min**) and then levels out. You come to the first *cava* — Pou de la Noguera. This large open cavern is 12m/40ft deep and just as wide.

The continuing path undulates above the left bank of the Barranco de las Zorras, and you can see it going up the slopes on the opposite bank. Fork right (**3h06min**) and cross the *barranco*, where a path comes in from the right (**3h08min**). *(The Alternative walk rejoins here.)*

Go straight up the other side to Cava Simarro (**3h 13min**). This 18th-century structure, the largest *cava* in this area, used to be the most beautiful, and has been partially restored. Above it are the ruins of a *casita*, but you should walk round the *cava* and up the slope, to a crest. From there you can see Ibi down in the valley, as well as the tiled roof in Arabian style of the well-preserved Cava Canyo, which you reach at **3h18min**. This is the smallest of the *cavas*; beside it are the ruins of the Casa Nevater ('Snowman's House').

From here the path widens to a rough track and heads towards Masía del Canyo, a *finca* in a small cultivated valley. As you approach it, you join a track coming in from the right. Go past the house and its *era* (**3h28min**). You are now on a wide path which passes along the top of the terracing, and heads down towards Ibi. Ignore minor hunters' paths; keep to the clear main trail. At a fork (**3h42min**), head left downhill. At a junction of many small paths, keep straight ahead on the wide main path (**3h48min**). When it sweeps sharp left, ignore a minor path straight ahead. Descend steeply, sometimes over large slab-like rocks. Zigzag down to a junction (**4h02min**; just beyond a large white-painted cairn with a hunting sign).

Here go straight ahead on a path marked with a PR post. You will realise from the still-visible hoof prints that this zigzag path, at times sculpted out of the rock, is the old mule trail down to Ibi from the *cavas* and the *finca*. Descend past almond groves until you join an asphalt road on the outskirts of town (**4h20min**). Follow the road past a metal fence and between terraces. Keep straight on, then go down steps to join your outward route to the town hall (**4h45min**).

You pass under this old aqueduct on the return to Penáguila (Walk 22).

22 PENAGUILA CASTLE

Distance: 6km/3.7mi; 1h53min   **See photograph opposite**

Grade: easy, except for the steep climb (230m/750ft) to the castle; one faint path which needs careful location

Equipment: see page 42

How to get there and return: 🚌 to/from Penáguila (the 41km-point on Car tour 4); park in the village.

Short walks (grade, equipment, access as above). Follow the main walk to the crest and back (2.5km/1.5mi; 1h08min) or to the castle and back (3km/1.9mi; 1h30min). You can shorten both of these walks even further by driving to Casa Alta (the 37km-point on Car tour 4): pick up the main walk at the 25min-point.

This walk, largely on pleasant paths, is short but well worthwhile. Penáguila Castle, with its origins in the 8th century, was reputedly a stronghold of the great Moorish leader Al Azraq. There have been some restorations over the years, but little now remains of the ruins. However, standing at the base of its walls, one can appreciate the strategic importance of its position.

The walk starts in the main church square. Facing the church, leave the square to the right. Go through a second square diagonally to the right, then head left up the main street, Carrer Verger de Patrocini. When it bears right, go straight ahead up some wide, shallow stone steps. Cross the main Alcolecha road and take the concrete road going up the hill. It climbs very steeply before crossing the Port de Tudons road (**5min**) and joining a narrow path about 10m/yds to the left. It runs alongside a small olive grove. This pretty path, with all the appearances of an old Moorish trail, climbs in zigzags, crossing the road twice more. Behind you, to the east, there are magnificent views of Serrella and, on the cliffs below the castle, many caves have been formed by the erosion of the soft rock.

The path ends as it joins the road once more (**24min**). Turn right and, on the first bend, reach the gates of Casa Alta (**25min**). Take the little path that goes up to the right of these gates. Ignore paths off to the left and keep climbing, as you wind around the Penáguila side of this hill, Cerro Castell. The narrow path is eroded in places. At a crest (**34min**; *P*22) the ruins of the castle come into view, a large cross towering above them. From here the surrounding sierras are spectacular, while Penáguila paints a pretty picture in the valley below. From here locate the indistinct path which descends to cross the rocks of the small saddle, below the ruins of an old tower. Take care as you pass the tower, and clamber up a steep path to the rest of the castle ruins (**46min**). Explore as you wish and

then retrace your steps to the asphalt road at Casa Alta (**1h05min**). From here you can either return along your outward route (turn left and walk back to your outward path, then follow it downhill to the left) or, for more variety, continue on the road to the first hairpin bend to the left (**1h15min**). Here a track goes straight ahead towards a small *casita* and some groves. Follow this track as it winds up through the groves. At **1h20min** an overgrown track can be seen going off to the left through pines. Follow this to a little path going right, some 20m/yds further on. Being indistinct, the first part is waymarked, but it soon becomes clear as it leads you down through pine woods, beside a *barranco*. After a steep section, you meet another path (**1h28min**): turn left and round the head of the *barranco*. Across the valley you will soon see the village of Benasau, nestled under the end of the Sierra de Serrella; below on your right, a track comes up from the village of Alcolecha. Your path passes above terraces and approaches, but does not meet, this track. The path eventually becomes a rough, rocky track as it descends towards Penáguila. It passes under an old aqueduct (photograph page 116) as it crosses a *barranco* (**1h 46min**). It then crosses the Penáguila-Alcolecha road and continues through the Jardí de Sants (a 'historic garden') and leads to some steps on the left. These take you up into the village. Turn left up a narrow street and reach the church square on the right (**1h53min**).

Walk 23 and Picnic 23a: Pou del Surdo from Carrasqueta Ridge

23 LA CARRASQUETA: PUERTO DE LA CARRAS-QUETA • POU DEL SURDO • MAS DE LA COVA • PUERTO DE LA CARRASQUETA

Distance: 14km/8.7mi; 3h55min   **See photograph opposite**

Grade: easy ascents and corresponding descents of 280m/920ft on good tracks and paths; navigation straightforward

Equipment: see page 42

How to get there and return: 🚌 or 🚐 from Alicante to the Puerto de la Carrasqueta on the N340 (the 144km-point on Car tour 4)

Short walks (equipment as page 42, access as above)

1 Pou del Surdo. 2.8km/1.7mi; 45min. Easy ascent/descent of 75m/250ft. Follow the main walk for 23min and return the same way.

2 Puerto de la Carrasqueta — La Sarga — N340. 9km/5.6mi; 2h40min. Easy ascents of 180m/590ft and descents of 280m/920ft. Follow the main walk to La Sarga (2h30min), then go directly to the N340 (less than 1km away), where you can catch a bus back to the Puerto or to Alicante.

With the starting point at 1024m/3360ft, this walk offers splendid panoramic views for a minimum of effort. The variety of terrain, from rugged hilltops to gentle cultivated valleys, and the wealth of interesting features to be seen en route, ensure enjoyment all the way.

Start out at the *mirador* on the right, at the top of the pass. Locate a rocky path going along the ridge from the car park. It takes you under electricity cables (**5min**) and joins a track, which soon splits. Take the right fork; it reduces to a rocky path (**10min**) which passes beneath a lone pine. From here you have a fantastic view down into the Jijona valley to the right. Walk through low, aromatic vegetation and pass a couple of large cairns, one with an old iron cross on it. At **23min** the Pou del Surdo, an old snow well at 1100m/3600ft, is a perfect picnic spot (***P**23a*). This well-preserved cylindrical *pou* (photograph opposite) is over 11m/36ft in diameter and roughly as deep. An iron ladder runs down the inside wall, and there is a mechanism for drawing up water.

From the *pou* the wide track will take you to some antennas (**28min**) and open up views to the left over the heavily-cultivated valley, with La Sarga at the far end. Follow the track as it passes the antennas and undulates, gradually gaining height. In this area you might disturb partridge, and you will surely see and hear the thekla larks. Ignore side tracks and climb to a junction (**45min**). Take the track off left, up an embankment, and continue to gain height. We have seen golden eagles soaring over the valleys to the right, so keep your eyes peeled. At the end of the ridge, a few metres/yards up to the right of the path, is the highest point on this branch of the Carrasqueta

Ridge (**1h03min**). It is only a minor peak (1200m/ 3940ft), but on top there is a cairn and a clump of Valencian oak trees. Surrounding views are impressive: the high peaks of Aitana with its antennas and Campana with its notch to the east; Cabezo de Oro to the southeast; Montcabrer, Alcoi and Cocentaina Castle (Walk 18) to the north. Continue on the same track, now badly eroded. Descend steeply, before contouring round to the saddle at the end of the ridge (**1h19min**). Climb past the head of a *barranco* on the left and, at about **1h26min**, before reaching a crest where there are two hunting signs, strike off left over open ground, to pick up the parallel track you can see about 100m/yds away. Turn left on this new track and head down a spur, with *barrancos* on both sides. Ignoring side tracks, descend gradually through Valencian oaks, high above the Sarga valley. As you emerge from the trees (**1h56min**), there is an open field to the left and a track going to the right.

Fork slightly left, passing Mas Plans de Baix, a farm off to the right. Wind round the edge of its fields to a fork (**2h03min**), where you keep right, through pines. Descend to the fields at the far side of the *mas,* and turn left on a wide track (**2h06min**). As you descend, notice some caves over on the rocky hillside to the right (**2h14min**); they house prehistoric cave paintings. On the left are the twin horns of the Carrasqueta Ridge. Reach an asphalt road (**2h20min**) at Mas de la Cova; the house is now uninhabited, but its terraces are still well cultivated. This is a good spot for a break (*P*23b) and, if you wish, you can walk up to the caves.

Then walk down the road, cross the stream bed, and climb the road straight ahead. *(But for Short walk 2 turn right to the N340.)* The road skirts to the left of the tiny village of La Sarga (**2h30min**). As you leave the houses behind, fork right on a dirt road. Then fork left (**2h36min**) on a track; at first it runs parallel with the track you just left, then it bends left between fields and through pines, up to a house (**2h46min**). Take the narrow path to the right of the house and continue past a small *casita* and a *lavadero*, up to a *font* in an open picnic area amongst some trees. Within the same complex, a bit further up, is the large Mas Els Pouets (**2h53min**). Leave the track for a closer look at this farm, with its own pretty chapel and

attractive surroundings (the chained dogs are quiet!). Then continue down to La Lloma, a collection of attractively-restored buildings. Go round past the front of the buildings (to the left) and climb a track, past a storage shed and through pines, to a three-way fork. Take the left-hand path and continue above the terraces to a T-junction (**3h09min**), where Mas del Fondo is signposted to the left. Turn right here, then go left immediately on an old trail. As you pass under electricity cables, cross a farm track and climb through trees. Go right at a fork (**3h15min**) and walk through some green gates, to the N340 (**3h20min**).

Cross the road diagonally to the right and go up the track past the fairly extensive, but ruined, Mas de Rovirá. The track winds up around terraces before settling in a direction parallel with the road. It descends to road level at a semi-cylindrical *pou*, still used as a well. A track continues past the *pou* but, when it sweeps right, you must head straight ahead across the open ground that borders the road. When a metal fence forces you down to the roadside, cross the road if you wish and continue for about 300m/yds, past another, enclosed *pou* on the right and back to the Puerto (**3h55min**).

24 ELDA • L'ARENAL • CAPRALA • RAMBLA DELS MOLINS • PETRER • ELDA

See map on reverse of touring map   See also photograph page 2

Distance: 18km/11.2mi; 5h (15.5km/9.6mi; 4h10min for motorists)

Grade: easy but long. Good tracks throughout; straightforward navigation

Equipment: see page 42

How to get there and return: 🚌 or 🚐 from Alicante to/from Elda railway station. By 🚗 take the exit from the N330 north of Elda (the 46km-point in Car tour 5) and turn right off this slip road for Petrer *before* crossing the *autovía*. Go under the slip road and park on the open ground close to three tunnels. Pick up the walk at the 40min-point.

Short walks (all are easy; equipment as above)

1 Rambla dels Molins. 1.6km/1mi; 35min. 🚗 Drive from Petrer or Elda to Restaurante Molino la Roja (the 94km-point on Car tour 5). Follow the main walk down the *rambla* from the 3h14min-point to the picnic spot (*P*24) — or as far as you like. Return the same way.

2 L'Arenal. 6km/3.7mi; 1h56min for those using public transport; 2km/1.2mi; 36min for motorists. Follow the main walk to the 58min-point and return the same way. Access as main walk.

Alternative walk: Elda to Castalla via the GR7. 19km/11.8mi; 5h20min. Moderate (ascent 600m/1970ft; descent 440m/1440ft). Equipment as above. Access: 🚌 or 🚐 from Alicante to Elda railway station. From Elda station, follow the main walk to the 2h23min-point. This is also the 2h28min-point on Walk 25. Take the GR track up to the left and follow the waymarks to Castalla (Walk 25 in reverse). In 4h50min you will reach the car parking point for Walk 25 and come to the bus stop in Castalla in 5h20min. *Note:* Just before Casa de Angel, a ruined hamlet above Castalla, you could take a very picturesque alternative route into Castalla by following Alternative walk 25-2 via the 'forgotten finca' shown on page 15. This would add about 30 minutes to your total time.

This is a lengthy, but mainly flat walk between sierras. Its two major points of interest are a huge inland sand dune and the Rambla dels Molins — a watercourse dotted with the ruins of many old mills.

The walk starts from the main exit of Elda station: turn right into Calle Galicia. Go straight ahead on the main road, under the railway lines. Cross the road immediately and locate some steps going down into Calle Río Segura. At the end of Calle Río Segura, scramble down the bank to the riverside and turn left along the canalised Río Viñalopó (**6min**). After going under a bridge and across a rough section, you must make a detour round a *casita* and enclosure (**15min**). From here the water is channelled underground and giant reeds grow in the bed. When the path runs out (**31min**) climb up a couple of terraces to the left and make for a small building close to the *autovía*. This bears red and white GR7 waymarks, which you will follow for some time. From here the river sweeps left under a road bridge, but you must take a track going right. You will see three tunnels ahead of you: go through any

L'Arenal: the local people claim that it is the only inland sand dune in Europe. It is certainly a very unusual sight, a rocky hill with one side completely covered in sand.

of them, under the *autovía* and up to a cross roads (**40min**). This is the parking place for motorists.

From the crossroads take the narrow waymarked asphalt road. Pass a long aqueduct; then, when the road forks right at a white wall (**48min**), take the unsurfaced road straight ahead, and fork right a couple of minutes later. Pass between houses with market gardens, almond and olive groves, and come level with the sandy hill shown above — L'Arenal (**58min**; *Short walk 2 turns back here*). From here a rough, rocky track takes you into the sierras. The GR waymarks are always present, if widely spaced. Skirting a wide *barranco,* you pass between the Sierra del Caballo on your right and Cabezo del Pino on your left. At a house (**1h11min**) ignore a track going up to the Sierra del Caballo. At **1h23min** ignore another track, with a chain across it, to a collection of houses. You reach an open area with tracks leading down into quarries; then, from the top of a rise, the mountain valley around the hamlet of Caprala opens out to the left.

At a junction of tracks next to a ruined *finca* (**1h34min**), take the track going down left. Cross the *barranco,* then resume the gentle climb into Caprala (**1h45min**), where the track becomes a narrow asphalt road. Follow it through the first part of the hamlet, which is mainly holiday homes, until another asphalt road goes obliquely right, down towards a bridge just below you. Follow it down, cross the bridge, then go straight ahead on a track (where the asphalt road continues to the right). Just past a distinctive red and white villa (where you will see the well shown on page 2), ignore a path coming down from the right to meet your track (**1h58min**). As you finally leave Caprala (**2h04min**), cross a *barranco* and, where the main track sweeps left, go straight ahead on a track signposted 'Via Pecuária' (pedestrian way). This badly-eroded track climbs through a narrow *barranco* for a few metres/yards. At the head of the *barranco*, a path takes you around a dam wall. Just after this (**2h09min**) ignore a track off right (PR waymarked) towards the Sierra del Caballo. Your (GR) track goes straight ahead, passing to the right of a large *finca* and cluster of houses. Continue straight ahead, ignoring side-tracks. But not far beyond the last building, at a junction (**2h23min**), leave the GR. *(Walk 25 comes in here, and the Alternative walk heads left uphill here with the GR, following Walk 25 in reverse.)* Continue on your track (no longer waymarked) as it bends to the right; ignore minor side-tracks. With pines on the left and groves on the right, you pass an electricity depot and come to a crossing of tracks (**2h39min**). Go straight across, now in open terrain with far-reaching views to Despeñador and the Sierra del Fraile in the east. As you round a right-hand bend, look left (southeast): beyond some deep and wide terraces, you can see the end of the Sierra del Fraile plunging dramatically into the Pantanet Gorge (Walk 25). Your track becomes a narrow asphalt road; it passes some houses in the Foieta de Racó and meets another road coming in from the left (**2h53min**).

Descend this quiet road through agricultural land. The Sierra del Caballo is still on your right. When the main road goes right towards Petrer (**2h59min**), keep left. After passing a house on the left, the asphalt gives way to rough track. Ignore a track going left to a second house . In spring there are all sorts of wild flowers here, and the resident serins are particularly noisy. The track joins an asphalt road at Restaurante Molina la Roja (**3h14min**).

Just below the restaurant lies the Rambla dels Molins, a mainly-dry river bed. It carries some water in winter and is liable to flash floods after wet weather — *take care!* Walk 25 continues from here up the *rambla*, but your route lies downstream to the right; so make your way into the river bed and enjoy a spectacular walk down to Petrer. The *rambla* is named after the water mills which used to grind the grain grown on surrounding terraces. Ruins of these mills remain alongside the *rambla*, and as you pick your way downstream — beside the watercourse or on a path along one of the banks — it is easy to imagine yourself in the past, leading your mules down this well-trodden route. As a path leads you left around the first of several (usually dry) waterfalls, don't stray up the track going left; take the path back down to the river bed. Cross it and continue along the opposite bank. The setting is spectacular as you walk under steep, sandy cliffs, with oleanders growing along the river bed (**3h30min**; *P*24).

Cross an asphalt road and continue along the water-course. The geological formations are fascinating, as well as spectacular, with mainly sandstone on the northern, sunny side of the gorge, and a variety of much harder rocks on the southern side. A track enters from the right opposite a partially-restored mill (**3h39min**). Behind it, other buildings are wedged into the hillside, some built into the cliff face, and a tunnel goes through the rock. Unfortunately it is all fenced off.

Another *rambla* comes in from the left at a point where there are almond groves in the river bed (**3h44min**). From **3h53min** an asphalt road runs on the left parallel with your route. Shortly after passing under some pipes, you enjoy an astonishing glimpse of Petrer Castle ahead. At the point where the castle is in full view, you reach an asphalt road (**4h08min**). Turn right and climb steeply up-hill. Meet the Petrer-Catí road (**4h13min**), turn left and continue all the way down to a major junction just before the *autovía* (**4h24min**).

If you parked by the tunnels, turn right uphill here (sign-posted to Aguarrios) for 100m/yds, then take the minor road left. This goes along the eastern side of the *autovía* (don't go under it to the left) and leads back to your car (**4h50min**). Those who came by bus or train should walk under the *autovía* and to the right of Continente hyper-market. At the roundabout, go straight ahead — all the way down Calle del Maestro Albeniz. Cross over and walk down the tree-lined path to the cemetery. Skirt to the right of the cemetery, then take a track straight ahead, across open ground. The main road is 50m/yds off to the right: join it and continue past another hypermarket, to a set of traffic lights at another large cemetery. Turn right downhill to a roundabout. Cross the road and take a minor asphalt road down towards the river and a sports complex. You will see two bridges. Head left, cross the river on the second bridge, and clamber up the bank to Calle Río Segura, ascending the steps at the end. In front of you is a railway bridge: turn left to the bus stop, or go under the bridge and turn left to Elda station (**5h**).

25 CASTALLA • FERMOSAS PLATEAU • PANTANET GORGE • CATI • DESPEÑADOR • CASTALLA

See map on reverse of touring map; see also photograph page 15

Distance: 31km/19.2mi; 8h50min (add 1h if travelling by bus)

Grade: strenuous, with ascents and corresponding descents of 1045m/ 3430ft. Mainly on good tracks, with only one or two rough sections. Ideal for a balmy winter's day (make an early start!). From April to October, it will probably be too hot to attempt the full walk, so we have split it into three Alternative walks, each lasting about 4 hours.

Equipment: see page 42; also compass and plenty of water

How to get there and return: 🚗 from Alicante to/from Castalla (the 76km-point on Car tour 5). Follow the touring notes (page 37) to the fork at 78km and go right. Park 300m further on, where an unsurfaced road goes right. Or 🚌 to/from Castalla. You will be dropped off in Calle Colón, at a bus shelter. Walk down Calle Colón (the bus also continues in this direction), then take the third turning right (Calle Azorín, later Oliveres). Walk to the end of the street, then turn left (red signpost to 'Xorret de Catí'). This road heads almost due south towards forested slopes. Fork right at about KM1.5, leaving the Catí road; then fork right again some 300m/yds further on, on an unsurfaced road. The walk starts at this fork, 30min from the bus stop in Castalla.

Short walk: 'Forgotten finca'. 6km/3.7mi; 1h40min. Access by 🚗 as above. Easy ascent/descent of 200m/650ft; equipment as page 42. Follow the main walk to the three-way junction (25min) Take the track furthest to the left; then, 5min later, turn right by a small building. Continue to the *finca* (*P* symbol on the map; *P*25a). Return the same way.

Alternative walks

1 Castalla — Elda. 16.8km/10.4mi; 5h20min. Fairly strenuous (climb 440m/1440ft; descent 600m/1970ft). Equipment as page 42. 🚌 from Alicante to Castalla; return by 🚌 or 🚆 from Elda station. See notes above to walk from the bus shelter in Castalla to the starting point (30min). Then follow the main walk to the 2h28min-point, where you go straight ahead on the GR7. This is also the 2h23min-point on Walk 24. Use the map to follow Walk 24 in reverse, from here to Elda station.

2 Castalla — Casa de Angel — 'forgotten finca' — Castalla. 8km/5mi; 2h36min (add 1h if travelling by bus). Moderate (climb/descent 410m/1345ft); equipment, access as main walk. Follow the main walk to the junction just after Casa de Angel (1h05min). Turn left up this rocky track. Climb to a crest, then descend into a dip (1h25min). Here another track goes downhill to the left, through thick pine woods. (From here you could take a 2h return detour to the summit of Despeñador: just continue along the ridge, enjoy the breathtaking views, and return to this point to continue.) Pick up the main walk notes at the 7h39min-point, to descend past the 'forgotten finca' and return to Castalla.

3 Fraile Ridge and Pantanet Gorge. 9.8km/6mi; 4h05min. Fairly strenuous, with climbs/descents of 500m/1640ft overall; you must be surefooted and have a head for heights. Equipment as main walk. 🚗 to/from Xorret de Catí (the 86km-point on Car tour 5, page 38). Pick up the main walk at the 5h38min-point and follow it to the 5h54min-point. Here continue left (signposted to the *mirador*), below sheer cliffs. Some 25min after setting out, fork right up to the *mirador*. From there climb a steep narrow path up to the right (clear PR waymarks). Then clamber on all fours up through a rocky cleft to a crest (40min; photograph opposite). From here a path leads right to the highest point on the Fraile Ridge

Alternative walk 3 is a spectacular hike, only recommended for the agile and vertigo-free. It traverses the long, narrow, crescent-shaped Fraile Ridge rising between Elda and Castalla (a different Fraile Ridge, near Bíar, is climbed in Walk 26). Set out on an April morning, when the valleys are alive with the call of the cuckoo.

(1211m/3970ft; 5min away) and on to Despeñador (a further 25min). But you should head *left*. Just after descending a little, the path comes close to the cliff edge, with fine views over El Cid and the Catí Valley (48min). Soon you will see the complete ridge stretching out before you, with Pantanet Gorge at the far end. The narrow path goes all the way along the edge of the cliff, past several posts and giant cairns. The route is PR waymarked from the opposite direction, so you will not notice the markers unless you look back. But you cannot get lost! The ridge is narrow, the drops are sheer, and you are going all the way to the gorge. As you approach the end of the ridge (2h18min), you begin to descend over bedrock. After passing the last cairn, locate a PR waymark on the rock on the right (north) side of the ridge, and another on a tree (both facing downhill). With your back to the tree, facing due west, start descending, keeping to the bedrock. There are more waymarks on the descent and, as the bedrock finishes, you will also see waymarks below in the gorge. Reach the gorge at a walkers' signpost and a *canaleta* (2h36min). This is the 4h09min-point on the main walk; pick up the notes and head left — through the gorge, past the Catí *ermita* and back to Xorret de Catí.

This extra-long walk covers part of the long-distance GR7. You follow wooded mountain tracks and then a rocky river bed through a deep gorge, to a spectacular dam. A country hotel provides a pleasant watering spot before you cross a high peak to return. Botanists will delight in the huge variety of wild flowers and plants to be seen in this area, particularly in spring.

Start out by following the wide unsurfaced road (red and white GR waymarks) uphill through olive and almond groves, towards the sierra. Fork left (**4min**), cross a stream and pass La Rambla, an enclosure on your left harbouring a motley collection of deer, barbary sheep and peacocks. Pass the last of the obvious houses ('Fam, Fum y Fret'; **15min**), where the road becomes a track. You have good views over the plain of Castalla to the left. Note a track going towards a quarry and an old lime kiln off to the right about 100m/yds away. Then pass two ruined houses, each one also with a kiln. The track sweeps round to the right at a three-way junction (**25min**). The track on the far left here is your return route *(and the route of the Short walk)*, but you go right following the GR waymarks. Pass the chained track to an abandoned *finca* on the right (**30min**). Steep crags rise above you. At **53min** you come to a faded sign to Finca Fermosa, and a chain across the road. Walk behind the chain and continue to the top of the sierra. The ruins of a *finca*, Casa de Angel, are on the right (**1h**). Although the building is in ruins, the terraces are still cultivated; this whole plateau is known as Fermosas.

As you continue on the track note a well down in a field on the right. The track off left just past this well (**1h05min**) leads along the ridge of the Sierra de Maigmó to Despeñador; it is your return route. *(Alternative walk 2 heads up left here.)* Continue through woodland across this high plateau, with the Sierra de la Argueña on the right. All the buildings up here are abandoned, but the plateau is still heavily cultivated. The GR7 forks right at a junction (**1h16min**), but you go *left*. (The GR inexplicably goes round two sides of a triangle, rejoining your track from the right at **1h26min**.) Ignore side-tracks as you begin to descend from the Fermosas plateau. The valley below opens out to the west, with views as far as the salt marshes beyond Elda, and to all the sierras stretching out in the distance. At **2h06min** a short-cut path down to the right cuts off a bend, but the main track is easier walking.

A track crosses yours as you reach more open terrain and the incline lessens (**2h13min**). The prominent flat top and twin peaks of El Cid dominate the skyline to the south. You are now walking through land belonging to the *finca* Costa o Novayal, visible on your right. Ignore tracks to the left and right. Two small cylindrical stone constructions are visible in the fields on the left. You pass under electricity cables by the second of these; a collection of buildings and a *finca* are ahead. After passing a chain barrier, but before reaching the first building, you come to a junction (**2h28min**). Turn left. *(Alternative walk 1 bears right here on the GR7, and Alternative walk 24 comes in here, en route to Castalla.)*

The next section of the walk is common to both this walk and Walk 24; pick up the notes for Walk 24 at the 2h23min-point (page 124), following this track past the electricity workers' depot. Follow Walk 24 as far as the

Restaurante Molino la Roja at the asphalt road (**3h19min**).

Below the restaurant is a river bed — Rambla dels Molins. Walk 24 follows this downstream to Petrer, but you turn left, upstream, walking on the flat rocks of the river bed for a short while. The *rambla* does contain some water throughout the winter, and after heavy rain there can be flash floods — so be aware. When you reach an asphalt road (**3h29min**), turn right, up towards Catí. The road sweeps round to the left (**3h38min**); then, just before a hairpin bend to the right, climb a track up right past Casa de la Loma, a small, inhabited *finca*. Just before the house, above you on the left, there is an excellent example of an *era* (grain-milling slab) and a millstone. The finca also has a dog, cunningly chained — so that you can only just get by out of its reach!

The track, now little more than a path, continues up the hill alongside almond groves and meets the asphalt road again (**4h**). Cross the road and locate a path, slightly to the left, with PR waymarkings; it leads through a pine wood. (There is a wider track going downhill alongside these groves, but your path begins to the right of this track and slightly higher up.) This path leads you into the spectacular Pantanet Gorge which you saw from the Foieta de Racó. Turn right and make your way over the rocks and up through the gorge, passing a signposted path coming down the rocks on your left, on the far side of a *canaleta* (**4h09min**). (Alternative walk 3 comes down here.) At the end of the gorge a huge dam wall towers above you (**4h16min**). It is an easy clamber up the rocks to the left, to join the continuation of the path; it takes you back to the asphalt road (**4h20min**).

This road continues left uphill to Catí, 3km away. But you must go right for about 300m/yds. Just opposite the entrance to Casa de Pantano, take the path to the left; it will take you up to the Collado de Moros. It's a steady climb up to this ridge, with lovely views of the craggy Sierra del Fraile to your left. Meet a track coming up from the valley on your right (**4h51min**) and turn left along it. It continues the gentle climb, then levels out. Pass a signposted footpath coming in from the right, before reaching the Catí *ermita*, a lovely spot for a break (**5h18min**; *P*25b). From the *ermita*, there are wonderful views across to El Cid and the Sierra de Maigmó to the south and east.

Leaving the *ermita* on the same track, you come to a junction: fork left downhill, passing Casa de la Administración off to the left, with a fine example of a *nevera* nearby.

(You pass a track off to it at **5h29min**, if you have time to visit.) Your track heads right and then turns right, joining a poorly-surfaced asphalt road to a modern hotel with excellent facilities — Xorret de Catí (**5h38min**).

From the hotel, take the asphalt road west towards Petrer, but after 100m/yds turn right towards the Mirador de Catí, on a wide track with PR waymarks. The crags of Despeñador tower above, as you climb steadily. Ignore side-tracks, including the one to Casa de la Coveta on the left. But when the track sweeps round to the left (sign-posted to the *mirador*), take the narrower track straight ahead (clear PR waymark; **5h54min**). *(But go left for Alternative walk 3.)* Fork left (**6h01min**) and, at a T-junction 200m/yds further on, turn left again on another track. This track curls round to an asphalt road, where you turn left. After about 100m/yds you will reach a crest, the Collado del Portell (**6h19min**), where there is a brick water deposit. Take the path up left alongside its fence; a steady climb brings you to the ridge below Despeñador (**6h34min**). Turn right to the summit with its triangulation marker (**6h40min**). The views from Despeñador are among the most spectacular we have seen in all of our walks in Alicante, with about 30 sierras being identifiable. It is absolutely breathtaking on a clear day.

Follow the clear track off the summit, initially going west and then northwest along the ridge. A track joins you from the right (from the Catí-Castalla road; **7h11min**). Ignore paths down into the valley on your left. When your track begins to drop sharply into a dip, in a small clearing (**7h39min**), look for a narrower, eroded track going down to the right and take it. *(Alternative walk 2 comes in here from Casa de Angel.)* At at fork (**7h49min**) go left. About six minutes later take a track running obliquely left; it contours round some terraces and suddenly reveals the old but substantial *finca* (**8h**) shown on page 15. Because it is located in such a secluded position and not named on any maps, we call it the 'forgotten finca' (**P**25a).

Just before reaching the *finca* you passed a track off right, alongside terraces. Take it now. Rough and rocky, it becomes a path which descends alongside a *barranco*. It widens out again and, at a junction near a *casita*, joins another track. Just before joining this track, turn left on a path going up behind the *casita* (**8h20min**). The path soon becomes a track and meets your outward route at the three-way junction (**8h29min**). Turn right downhill, past the lime kilns and to your starting point (**8h50min**).

26 SIERRA DEL FRAILE AND CAMI DE SAN JUAN

Map on reverse of touring map   **Distance:** 12km/7.4mi; 3h30min

Grade: moderate, with ascents and corresponding descents of 470m/ 1540ft; navigation straightforward throughout

Equipment: see page 42

How to get there and return: 🚌 to the 29km marker on the A211 between Sax and Castalla (the 67km-point on Car tour 5). A track leaves the road to the north here, with space to park just above road level.

Short walk: Camí de San Juan. 5km/3mi; 1h30min. Easy (climb/descent 170m/560ft). Equipment and access as above. Follow the main walk to the 41min-point, then fork right. In about 5min you come to a forestry road: turn right and follow the main walk from the 2h50min-point to the end.

A major summit, an interesting old trail, and fantastic views all contribute to the magic of this walk. Located in one of the cooler parts of the region, the almond trees blossom later here than elsewhere, making this a perfect walk for a warm day in mid-March.

Start the walk by going up the track where you parked, past a large 'Serra de Bíar' sign. Ignore a track to the left (**3min**) and continue to a small cultivated field (**9min**). Just past the field take a narrow path marked by cairns into pine woods on the right. This is the first stage of an old trail, its origins shrouded in mystery. We have called it the Camí de San Juan, after the *font* further up. This narrow rocky trail climbs gradually, clearly marked with cairns, towards the crags of Biar's Sierra del Fraile. (Alternative walk 25-3 follows the crest of a different Sierra del Fraile, rising between Castalla and Elda.)

After crossing the sandy bed of a small *barranco,* in **15min** you reach the first of several hunting reserve boundary markers (**19min**), overlooking an almond grove (*P*26). At **25min** join a track and turn left towards the ridge. (The return route comes in from the right.) Turn left on reaching a forestry road (**34min**), but after 50m/yds leave it: take the track up to the right. (First you might like to look at the well by the

Camí de San Juan

roadside, just beyond the track.) This track heads towards the summit of Fraile, but ends at an open area — a resting spot for hunters. From here take a small path up to the right. When it forks (**41min**), go left. *(The Short walk goes right here.)* A few minutes later meet a pebbly *barranco*. Walk up the *barranco* bed for about 50m/yds; the path becomes obvious again, and takes you off to the left. Continue beside the *barranco*, with the Sierra del Fraile rising on either side. Some cairns dot this rocky path. The way steepens as it bends to the right and brings you to the Font de San Juan (**1h06min**) — unfortunately locked.

Catch your breath, then continue uphill. After leaving the tree line, you reach the path along the ridge (**1h18min**). Continue right for 100m/yds, to the summit and trig point (1042m/3420ft). After taking in the fine views to the left across the heavily-cultivated Bíar Valley and to the right over the Sax Valley, continue past the summit. Some 200m/yds along, head steeply down right over the rocks (a cairn marks this path). On reaching the tree line, the path becomes a rough track and levels out for a while. When it descends once more, take care on the loose rocky surface, and pause to admire the rocky crags on the left.

The track takes you down into a dip (**1h40min**), then crosses a pine-filled valley before rising again, past old terraces, to a crest (**1h46min**). Ignore a track to the left here, but notice the unusual rock formations in that direction. Your track bears right and descends past some interesting old stone distance markers to a junction (**1h 49min**). Here there is an antenna alongside the fairly extensive ruins of Casa del Fraile, and a good view down into Bíar, overlooked by its prominent castle.

Take the right-hand track, and turn right when you reach a forestry road (**1h55min**). Good views over the valley to the left accompany you on your steady climb to the highest point (**2h26min**) and your gradual descent. At **2h50min** you will see a path coming in from the right, along the edge of a small cultivated patch of ground. *(The Short walk rejoins here.)* After winding down through three hairpin bends, watch for your track off to the left (**2h56min**). It is marked with a cairn, and there is a red marker on the rocks opposite. Lined with rosemary, it meanders pleasantly through pines to a crossing of tracks beside extensive almond groves (**3h04min**). Turn right; then, about 100m/yds after crossing a small *barranco*, a cairn on the left marks your narrow outward path. Follow it back past the picnic spot, to your car (**3h30min**).

BUS AND TRAIN TIMETABLES

Albir–Benidorm; Bus N° 6; daily; journey time 25min

Departs Albir 0855, 0955, 1055, 1155, 1255, 1355, 1555, 1655, 1755, 1855, 1955, 2055

El Trenet ('Lemon Express') narrow gauge railway Alicante–Denia; daily

Alicante	0600	0800	1000	1300	1500	1700	1900
Villajoyosa	0651	0851	1051	1351	1551	1751	1951
Benidorm	0708	0908	1108	1408	1608	1808	2008
Calpe	0737	0937	1137	1437	1637	1837	2037
Denia	0817	1017	1217	1517	1717	1917	2117
Denia	0625	0825	1025	1325	1525	1725	1925
Calpe	0707	0907	1107	1407	1607	1807	2007
Benidorm	0736	0936	1136	1436	1636	1836	2036
Villajoyosa	0752	0952	1152	1452	1652	1852	2052
Alicante	0842	1042	1242	1542	1742	1942	2142

Alicante–Villajoyosa–Benidorm (Avenida Europa)–Calpe–Jávea–Denia (UBESA bus company); daily, except where noted

		NS		NS			NSS	
Alicante		0630	0800	0900	1100	1230	1300	1400
Villajoyosa		0710	0840	0940	1140	1310	1340	1440
Benidorm		0725	0855	0955	1155	1325	1355	1455
Calpe		0805	0935	1035	1235	1405	1435	1535
Jávea	0745	—	1020	—	—	1450	—	—
Denia	0815	0900	—	1130	1330	—	—	1630
	NSS				NS		NS	
Alicante	1500	1600	1700	1800	1900	2000	2100	
Villajoyosa	1540	1640	1740	1840	1940	2040	2140	
Benidorm	1555	1655	1755	1855	1955	2055	2155	
Calpe	1635	1735	1835	1935	2035	2135	2235	
Jávea		1820	—	—		2215	—	
Denia	1730	—	1930	2025	2125	—	2325	

	NS	NS		NS				
Denia	—	—	0730	—	0950	1120	—	1420
Jávea	—	0645	—	0840	—	—	1315	—
Calpe	0725	0725	0825	0920	1040	1210	1355	1510
Benidorm	0805	0905	1005	1120	1250	1435	1550	
Villajoyosa	0820	0920	1020	1140	1305	1450	1605	
Alicante	0825	0900	1000	1100	1220	1345	1530	1645
	NSS							
Denia	1600	—	1750	—	2020			
Jávea	—	1700	—	1915	—			
Calpe	1650	1740	1840	1955	2105			
Benidorm	1730	1820	1920	2035	2145			
Villajoyosa	1745	1835	1935	2050	2200			
Alicante	1825	1915	2015	2130	2240			

NS not Sundays; **NSS** not Saturdays or Sundays

Alicante–Alcoi, via Jijona and the Puerto de la Carrasqueta (Alcoyana Bus Co)*

Departs Alicante (passes the Puerto de la Carrasqueta 40min later)
Mon–Fri	0800	1000	1130	1300	1400	1630	1800	2100	
Sat	0800	1130	1330	1630	1800	2100			
Sun	0800	0900	1330	1600	1800	2100			

Departs Alcoi (passes the Puerto de la Carrasqueta 20min later)
Mon–Fri	0630	0800	0945	1200	1330	1530	1800	1930	
Sat	0630	0945	1200	1330	1630	1930			
Sun	0700	0945	1330	1530	1800	1930			

*See also next timetable (Alicante–Alcoi via Castalla)

Alicante–Alcoi via Castalla (journey time to Castalla 45min)*

Departs Alicante (arrives Castalla 45min later)

Mon-Sat	0900	1330	2000
Sun	1130	2000	

Departs Alcoi (arrives Castalla 30min later)

Mon-Sat	0645	1100	1700
Sun	0900	1700	

See also previous timetable, Alicante–Alcoi via the Puerto de la Carrasqueta

Benidorm–Guadalest (journey time 40min)

Departs Benidorm	Hotel Bali	Railway station	Calle Esparanto	Rincón de l'Oix
	0845	0900	0910	0915
	1515	1530	1540	1545
Departs Guadalest	1230			
	1900			

Ontinyent–Bocairent (journey time 20min)

Departs Ontinyent

Mon-Fri	1000	1230	1800	2015
Sat	1300			
Sun/holidays	no service			

Departs Bocairent

Mon-Fri	0815	1030	1615	1830
Sat	0730			
Sun/holidays	no service			

Muro de Alcoi–Cocentaina–Alcoi (from Muro centre; journey time to Cocentaina 10min; journey time to Alcoi 20min)

Departs Muro

Mon-Sat	1230	1330	1630	1730	1830	1930
Sundays	1200	1300	1600	1700	1800	1900

Alicante–Elda, *buses*
(ALSA Bus Co; final destination Villena; journey time 40min)

Departs Alicante	0900	1000	1100**					
Arrives Elda station	0940*	1040*	1140**					

Departs Elda station

Mon-Fri	1400	1500	1600	1700	1800	1900	2000	2100
Sat	1500	1600	1800;	1900				
Sundays/holidays	1535	1635	1855	1935 (takes 1h10min)				

*20 minutes later on Sundays; **runs Mon-Fri only

Alicante–Elda, *trains*

Departs Alicante	0824	Arrives Elda	0905
Departs Elda	1702	Arrives Alicante	1743
	2034 (Fridays only)		2100

 Index

Geographical names comprise the only entries in this index. For other entries, see Contents, page 3. A page number in **bold type** indicates a photograph; a page number in *italic type* a map (*TM* refers to the large-scale *walking map* on the reverse of the touring map). Both may be in addition to a text reference on the same page. Mountains and snow wells are grouped separately under those headings.